AF413640

A GENEALOGY OF THE CROSSMAN FAMILY
Descendants of John and Robert Crossman of Taunton, Massachusetts
Supplement #2

Including the Ancestry and Descendants
of
Asa Croasmun/Crossman
of Cherry Tree, Indiana County, Pennsylvania 1765-1828
not available when the 1977 edition or the 1982 supplement were published

Compiled
by
Robert Owen Crossman

*Information in this supplement was not available when the 1977 edition or the 1982 supplement
were published and therefore does not duplicate those volumes of Crossman Genealogy.
A great word of appreciation is due to Marion Croasmun, Dale Croasmun, Barbara Silveira
and Alfred Denman who have faithfully collected records
of births, death, and marriages through the years.*

Ingram Spark Press
ISBN 978-0-9996578-1-2

13

JOHN CROSMUN
b. 1588 - d. 1688

ROBERT CROSSMAN, Son of John Crosmun
b. 1622 - d. 1692

Sarah   John   Mary   Robert   Joseph   Samuel   Mercy   Thomas   Susanna
b. 1653   b.1657   b. 1659   a.1. Elizabeth   a. John Thraser   Killed in war   b.1673
                                    d. 1738   d. 1696   2. Margaret Sayer   (Eight children)   with Canada.   d.1696
                                    a. Hannah Brooks a. Sarah Alden *   3. Anna Case
                                                                4. Mary Jones

                                                                *(John Alden, b.1599 - d. 1687, a. Priscilla Mullens, d. 1650
                                                                Joseph Alden, son of John Alden, a.Mary Simmons
Joseph   Sarah   Mary   Lydia   Sarah Alden, daughter of Joseph Alden, a. Joseph Crossman.)
b. 1690
d. 1776 or 1777
a.(1)Deborah Pratt -   (2)Elizabeth Washburn

Washburn

Elizabeth   Joseph   William   Daniel   James (Croasman)   Deborah   Abigail   Mary
b. 1717   b. 1718   b. 1718   b. 1720   b. 1721   a. Seth Pratt
            d. 1776 or 1777   a.(1)Sarah Riford   (2)Mary Priest -
            a. Mary Carey
                                                                                                    **(Peter Oliver, a. Susannah Sole,
                                                                                                    Joseph Oliver, son of Peter, a. Ann Russell
                                                                                                       b.1706
                                                                                                       d.1790
                                                                                                       Joseph Oliver, son of Joseph, a. Dority Petis
                                                                                                          b. 1739
                                                                                                          Patience Oliver, daughter of Joseph and Dority,
                                                                                                             a. Asa Crossman)

James   Sarah   Asa   Eunice   Elijah   Johnathin
b. 1746   b. 1765   Died young.
d. 1838   d. 1828
a. Rebecca Proctor   a. Patience Oliver**
   b. 1764
   Icabod
      a. Susannah Harris
      (Palermo, NY)

Chloe   Asa   Rebecca   Joseph   Oliver   Nathan   William
b. 1792, NH b. 1794, NH b. 1796, NH   b. 1798, NH   b. 1800, NH   b. 1804, NY   a. Eva Hostler
            a. Mary McHenry a. John Piper   a. Catherine McHenry   a. (1) Catherine Foster
                            Rebecca Piper   (2) Rachel O'Hara
                              a.Winfield Neal
                                Elizabeth Neal
                                  a. William Asa Croasman

Cyrus   Mary   Isaac   Nathan   Asa   Miles   James   Elizabeth   William
            b. 1823   b. 1824   b. 1826   b. 1828   b. 1831   b. 1833
                                    a. Mary Blose

ACKNOWLEDGEMENTS

Credit for this supplement goes to Marion Croasmun, Barbara Silveira, Dale Croasmun, and Alfred Denman who have faithfully collected records of births, deaths, and marriages through the years. Dale Croasmun and Barbara Silveira are also to be commended for their deligent search for the parentage of Asa Croasmun of Cherry Tree, Pennsylvania.

LIST OF REFERENCE FOOTNOTES

(AA)	*American Ancestry*, Volume iv, page 197
(AD)	Alfred M. Denman, 6514 N.Regal Street,Spokane,Wash.99207
(BBB)	Buel Burdett Bassett, *One Bassett Family in America*.
(BCP)	Bristol County Probate Record, as quoted in (EC).
( )	*The Boston Transcript*, October 3, 1910
(BS)	Barbara Silveira, 6839 Colton Blvd.,Oakland,Calif. 94611
(BV)	Bridgewater, Mass. Vital Records as quoted in (EC).
(CP)	From papers relating to the Crossman family in the possession of the Old Colony Historical Society of Taunton, Mass. as quoted in (EC).
(DC)	Dale Croasmun 202 Sunset Dr., Cumberland,MD 21502.
(EC)	Edgar Leonard Crossman, *Genealogy of the Crossman Family from Robert Crossman of Dedham and Taunton*, unpublished, about 86 pages, kept at the Old Colony Historical Society, 66 Church Green, Taunton, Mass. 02780.
(EM)	Emery's *History of Taunton*, as quoted by (EC).
(EMs)	S.H. Emery's *History of Taunton Supplement*.
(EV)	Easton, Mass. Vital Records, as quoted in (EC).
(FBW)	Flora B. Weeks #7 Marble Ave., Rutland, VT 05701
( )	Journal of the 61st Session of the California Conference held on September 17, 1913 (Methodist) as quoted by (BS).
(MAC)	Margaret Allan Crossman, *Genealogy of the Crossman Family 1637-*, compiled from a notebook kept by Warren N. Howard, the 133 page unpublished manuscript is located at the Huntington Historical Society, Huntington, Long Island, New York.
(MC)	Marion Crossman, P.O. Box 72 Valier,Penn including a family group sheet provided by Barbara Silveira 9/24/76.
(OC)	Old Colony Historical Society, Taunton, Mass.
( )	"Oregonian", March 17, 1926 provided by (BS).
(TPR)	Taunton Proprietor's Records, as quoted by (EC).
(TV)	Taunton Vital Records, as quoted by (EC).
(WC)	Rev. William L. Chaffin, *History of Easton, Massachusetts*.
(WOC)	Ward Olin Crossman, "*Genealogy of some of the Crossman families in Massachusetts....*", 1961,1964,1966,1969.

471

TABLE OF CONTENTS

This supplement is dedicated to my mother,
Roberta Francis Crossman,
who died on Thursday July 9, 1981.

PREFACE

In the 1977 volume of <u>A GENEALOGY OF THE CROSSMAN FAMILY,</u>
<u>Descendants of John and Robert Crossman of Taunton, Massachusetts,</u>
the introduction stated, "...genealogy is a continous process...
findings though incomplete should be published so that a permanent
record...be available to both present and future Crossman family
researchers." It is in this same spirit that this second supplement
is offered.

This supplement to the 1977 volume is essentially a reproduction
of the author's genealogical notebook. The format allows the reader
to have a permanent record of the latest Crossman family research
without having to wait years until the project is completed. The
author intends to publish supplements periodically until enough
data has been gathered to merit another complete edition some years
in the future.

This supplement contains additional material, with little
repetition of data found in the 1977 volume or the 1982 supplement.

No numbers are assigned to names in this supplement except for
a generation number. In reference to the author, 'Robert-11 Crossman'
would show that Robert was in the eleventh generation of descendants
of John Crossman of Taunton, Massachusetts. To identify Robert more
accurately, we would list his ancestry back to John: (Robert-11,
Paul-10, Nelson-9, Samuel-8, Samuel-7, Samuel-6, Stephen-5, Nathaniel-4,
Robert-3, Robert-2, John-1). This allows a reconstruction of
Robert's ancestry even if the 1977 volume is not available to fill
in the details. This method is dictated by the inevitable fact
that these supplements will often be seperated from the 1977
volume. This method also makes it possible to see Robert's ancestry
'at a glance' without having to trace all the numbers back through
several volumes.

If any readers have additional material not found in this
supplement, please forward the data to the compiler of this
genealogical collection of Crossman family history:

Dr. Bob Crossman
8 Sternwheel Drive
Conway, AR 72034-9391

Copies of Volume 1 and Supplement #1 are also available from the author.

Apr.   Month of April
Aug.   Month of August
b.   date of birth
Bp.   date of baptism
d.   date of death
dau.   Daughter
Dec.   Month of December
Feb.   Month of February
Jan.   Month of January
Jr.   Junior. A son with same name as his father.
Jun.   Junior. A son with same name as his father.
L   Pounds - the monetary unit of the United Kingdom
L 1-9-8   One Pound, nine shillings, and eight pennies
m.   date of marriage
m(1)   date of first marriage
m(2)   date of second marriage
m.int.   date intention to marry was posted, usually occured
              about two weeks prior to actual marriage date.
Mar.   month of March
Nov.   month of November
Oct.   month of October
s.   son
Senr.   Senior. A male with a son of the same name.
Sept.   month of September
Sr.   Senior. A male with a son of the same name.
(   )   Date unknown. example: m.(   ) John Doe.
_____   Name unknown. example: m.Aug.1,1756 John ________.
****   End of material on person being discussed. This usually
              follows a list of the children's names.
Number

474

Genealogy of the Crossman Family, Supplement #3 · ©1990 by Robert Owen Crossman · 908 Front · Conway, AR 72032

Our
First
Generation

Genealogy of the Crossman Family, Supplement #3 • ©1990 by Robert Owen Crossman • 906 Front Street • Conway, Arkansas 72032

see page 1-4, 222-226

JOHN-1 CROSSMAN

    b. about 1588 (BBB)
    d. Jan. 26, 1688 at Newport, Rhode Island (BBB)
    m. no record available

    CHILDREN:

see page
478
ROBERT-2 CROSSMAN, b.possibly about 1622 in England (AA)
    d. Oct. 1692 (BBB); or 1690 (Em-87) or 'before 1675'(TPR)
    m(1) May 25, 1652 Sarah Kingsbury in Dedham, daughter of
        Joseph and Millicent (Ames) Kingsbury of Dedham,
        she died in 1686 (CP)
    m(2) 1687 Mrs. Martha Easton or Eatton of Bristol,
        Massachusetts, widow of Samuel Easton, and daughter
        of Francis Billington (EMs-8), Bristol is now in
        Rhode Island, she died in 1695 (CP).

"John Crossman....settled in Taunton, Mass., in 1638 or 39.
He came from Southwestern England but from just what locality
is not certain. One Theory is that the family originated in
Somersetshire, descendants of Lawrence Crossman, Gent. -
another that the surname first came into use as a 'place-name'
from a village or cross (crossroads) in Cornwall. Recent
research in England makes it clear that one or more Crossman
families were established near Bodmin, Cornwall, before John
came to America...." (WOC-L. of D.2)

"He is believed to have come a widower, aged about 51 or 52,
bringing with him his son Robert." (WOC-L. of D.2)

"There has been some controversy as to whether John or Robert
Crossman was the originator of the Crossman family that
figured in Taunton, Massachusett's early history...."(FBW)

"The fact that John Crossman is given by Savage as the father
of Robert leads me to consider Robert the second generation in
America and John the first..." (FBW)

For a fuller account of the records available on John, see
pages 1 through 4, and 222 through 226 in A Genealogy of
the Crossman Family, Descendants of John and Robert Crossman
of Taunton, Massachusetts printed in 1977; and A Genealogy
of the Crossman Family, Descendants of John and Robert Crossman
of Taunton, Massachusetts, Supplement #1 printed in 1982.

****

Our
Second
Generation

Genealogy of the Crossman Family, Supplement #3 • ©1990 by Robert Owen Crossman • 905 Front Street • Conway, Arkansas 72032

see page 4-9, 228-239,   see page
476

ROBERT-2 CROSSMAN   (Robert-2, John-1)

b. possibly about 1622 in England (AA)
d. Oct. 1692 (BBB); or 1690 (Em-87); or 'before 1675'(TPR)
m(1) May 25, 1652 Sarah Kingsbury in Dedham, daughter of
        Joseph and Millicent Ames Kingsbury of Dedham, she
        died in 1686 (CP).
m(2) 1687 Mrs. Martha Easton or Eatton of Bristol, Massachusetts,
        widow of Samuel Easton, and daughter of Francis
        Billington (Ems-8), Bristol is now in Rhode Island,
        she died in 1695 (CP).

    CHILDREN: (all by first wife)

SARAH-3 CROSSMAN, b. 1653 in Dedham (CP)
   d. 1688
   m. Nov.11,1675 John Woodward of Taunton and Plymouth,
        he died May 10, 1688 (CP)(BBB); married at Rehoboth
        (WOC-L. of D.2) son of Nathaniel and Katherine
        Woodward (FBW)
        See page 242 for her descendants.
JOHN-3 CROSSMAN, b. March 16, 1654 (TPR) at Taunton(WOC-L D2);
   d. Dec. 1731 (BBB) about 1730 (CP) May 18,1727 (WOC-L of D.2);
   m. Jan.7,1690 Joanna Thayer, daughter of Nathaniel Thayer
        of Taunton (TV); at Taunton (WOC-L of D.2);
        Jan. 7, 1685 (MAC-2).
        See page 10 and 243 for his descendants.
MARY-3 CROSSMAN, b. July 16, 1655 (TPR) at Taunton (WOC-L+D2);
    d.
   m. Aug. 21, 1673 (BBB) or Aug. 24,1673 at Taunton(WOC-L D2)
        or Aug. 24, 1685 (MAC-2) John Gould of Tauton, he died
        Dec. 14, 1711 (BBB).
        See page 256 for her descendants.
ROBERT-3 CROSSMAN, b.Aug.3,1657(TPR) at Taunton (WOC-L D2);
   d. about 1738 (CP); aged 81 years (CP);
   m. July 21, 1679 Hannah Brooks, daughter of Gilbert
        Brooks of Rehoboth (CP) and Elizabeth Brooks (FBW)
        See pages 11-13 and 241 for his descendants.
see page
481 JOSEPH-3 CROSSMAN, b. April 25,1659 (TPR) at Taunton(WOC-L D2);
        d. March 17, 1775 , buried in Easton, Church Street
        Cemetary (WC); or before 1713 (CP); or died before
        June 29, 1693 (EC);
   m. Nov. 24,1685 Sarah Alden (TV) at Taunton (WOC-L D2);
        of John Alden (CP); daughter of Mary Simmons Alden(FBW).
NATHANIEL-3 CROSSMAN, b.Aug. 7, 1660 (TPR) at Taunton (WOC-1);
   d. March 8, 1676 killed by Indians at Wrentham, Mass (CP).
ELEAZER or ELEAZOR-3 CROSSMAN, b.March 16,1663 (TPR)May 16,1664(MA
   d. Oct. 26, 1667 (TPR) at Taunton (WOC-L D 2)
ELIZABETH-3 CROSSMAN, b. May 2, 1665 (TPR) at Taunton (WOC)
   d. Dec. 26, 1739 in East Bridgewater (CP)
   m. Nathaniel Hayward, he was prob. born April 26,1664 (BV);
        See page 247 for her descendants.

                              continued.........

continued from previous page:

SAMUEL-3 CROSSMAN, b. July 25, 1667(TPR) at Taunton(WOC);
   d. May 1, 1755 (BBB)
   m(1) Dec. 19, 1689 Elizabeth Bell, daughter of James
          Bell (TPR), she was born Nov. 15, 1668 (TPR);
          or married Dec. 19, 1682 (MAC-3);
   m(2) Dec. 26, 1696 Widow Mary Sawyer Gulliver (BBB-27);
          or Mary Sawyer (TPR);
   m(3) Sept. 22, 1739 (BBB) Dec. 16, 1692 (MAC-3) Anna
          Case (CP) at Taunton (WOC-L D 2);
   m(4) Mrs. Mary Joanes, widow of Thomas Joanes (CP).
          See page 14-15 and 248 for his descendants.
MERCY-3 CROSSMAN, b. March 20, 1669 (TPR)
   d.
   m. Jan. 26, 1687 John Trasher (TPR) of Taunton (MAC)
        he was born Dec. 8, 1653 (AD).
THOMAS-3 CROSSMAN, b. Oct. 6, 1671 (TPR)
   d. 1690 (BBB) enlisted in Captain Gallup's Company
        in Sir William Phipps expedition to Canada and was
        killed (Em-87).
SUSANNA-3 CROSSMAN, b. Feb. 14, 1673 (TPR); Feb.11,1672(MAC-3);
   d. before 1696 unmarried (CP).

For lengthy material on Robert-2 Crossman see pages 4
through 9 in <u>A GENEALOGY OF THE CROSSMAN FAMILY</u>, 1977
and pages 228 through 239 in <u>A GENEALOGY OF THE CROSSMAN
FAMILY, SUPPLEMENT #1</u>, 1982.

Genealogy of the Crossman Family, Supplement #3 · ©1990 by Robert Owen Crossman · 908 Front · Conway, AR 72032

**This page is intentionally blank
to allow the next generation
to begin on a right hand page.**

Our
Third
Generation

see pages 13-14 and 241 and see page 478

JOSEPH-3 CROSSMAN   (Joseph-3, Robert-2, John-1)

b. April 25, 1659 (TPR) at Taunton (WOC-L D of 2);
d. March 17, 1775, buried in Easton, Church Street
   Cemetary (WC); or died before 1713 (CP); or died
   before June 29, 1693 (EC).
m. Nov. 24, 1685 Sarah Alden (TV) at Taunton (WOC-L of D2);
   of John Alden (CP);daughter of Mary Simmons Alden(FBW).

CHILDREN:

see page 483

JOSEPH-4 CROSSMAN, b. 1690 ; 1688 (EC);
   d. Feb. 9, 1775, buried in the oldest cemetary of
      Easton called the Church Street Cemetary (WC) or
      died March 17, 1775 (OC); March 14, 1776 at
      Easton (WOC-A);
   m.(1) March 8, 1716 Deborah Pratt of Easton, she died
         May 4, 1731 (CP);
   m.(2) Aug. 20, 1742 Elizabeth Leonard Washburn (CP);
         or Aug. 20, 1752 (EV)(CP), widow of James Washburn
         and daughter of Josiah Leonard, she died Oct.
         14, 1782 or 1783 in her 81st year (BV).

SARAH-4 CROSSMAN, b.
   d.
   m. Sept. 9, 1703 Joseph Hayward, Jr. at Bridgewater,
      Mass.
   See page 14 for her descendants.

MARY-4 CROSSMAN, b. possibly April 17, 1691 (BV)
   d. 1726
   m. Dec. 25, 1711 Recompence Cary, deacon;
      at Bridgewater (WOC-A); he married 2nd, Sarah
      Alden Brett on Jan. 17, 1727 (FBW).

LYDIA-4 CROSSMAN, b.
   d.

****

Our
Fourth
Generation

see page 17 and 18 and see page 481

JOSEPH-4 CROSSMAN   (Joseph-4, Joseph-3, Robert-2, John-1)

    b. 1690 ; 1688 (EC);
    d. Feb. 9, 1775, buried in the oldest cemetary of Easton called the Church Street Cemetary (WC) or died March 17, 1775 (OC); March 14, 1776 at Easton (WOC-A) (FBW).
    m(1) March 8, 1716 Deborah Pratt of Easton, she died May 4, 1731 (CP);
    m(2) Aug. 20, 1742 Elizabeth Leonard Washburn (CP); or Aug. 20, 1752 (EV)(CP), widow of James Washburn and daughter of Josiah Leonard, she died Oct. 14, 1782 or 1783 in her 81st year (BV).

    CHILDREN:

ELIZABETH-5 CROSSMAN, b. Feb. 24, 1717 (CP);
    d.
    Edgar Crossman records the name ELEAZER for this birth instead of Elizabeth (EC-3-2)(EV), named ELIZER (FBW).

JOSEPH-5 CROSSMAN, b. Sept. 15, 1718 (CP);
    d. Feb. 9, 1775 and is buried in the same lot as his father in the Church Street Cemetary in Easton; or died before Sept. 16, 1776 when his property was distributed;
    m(1) Feb. 18, 1747 Mary Cary (CP) daughter of Recompense and Mary Crossman Cary in East Bridgewater (FBW);
    m(2) Feb. 26, 1756 (FBW)(EC) Margaret Turner.

WILLIAM-5 CROSSMAN, b. Sept. 15, 1718 (CP).
    d.

DANIEL-5 CROSSMAN, b. Oct. 20, 1720 (CP);
    d.

see page 485
JAMES-5 CROSSMAN, b. July 20, 1721 (CP);
    d.
    m. Sarrah________, June 18, 1745 (EC); Sarrah Ryfard in 1745/46 (DC).

SARAH-5 CROSSMAN, b. July 20, 1721 (CP)
    d.
    m. June 21, 1770 Ebenezer Harring of Dedham (CP).

DEBORAH-5 CROSSMAN, b. March 13, 1728 in Easton (CP);
    d. March 11, 1805 in Norton (CP);
    m. Nov. 1, 1750 David Lincoln, of Norton, son of Samuel and Hannah Lincoln (CP); he died July 20, 1822 in Norton (CP).
    For her descendants see page 279.

ABIGAIL-5 CROSSMAN, b.

MARY-5 CROSSMAN, b.

Our
Fifth
Generation

Genealogy of the Crossman Family, Supplement #3 • ©1990 by Robert Owen Crossman • 908 Front Street • Conway, Arkansas 72032

see page 18   see page
483

JAMES-5 (#73) CROASMAN/CROSSMAN   (Joseph-4, Joseph-3, Robert-2,
                                          John-1)

    b. July 20, 1721 (CP).
    d.

    m. Sarrah ________, June 18, 1745 (EC); Sarrah Ryfard in
       1745/46 (DC).

      CHILDREN:

JAMES-6 CROASMAN, b. March 2, 1746 (DC).
   d.
  m. Mary Priest in Haldeston (DC).

      CHILDREN

         EUNICE-7 CROASMAN, b.
           d.
           m. George Conant (DC); they lived 10 miles from
              her uncle, Asa-6 Croasmun in Hanover (DC).

         ELIJAH-7 CROASMAN, b. "possible son of James Jr." (DC)

see page
488 ASA-6 CROASMUN, b. 1765 (DC).
      d. "tombstone spells last name 'Croasmun'" (DC).
      m. Patience Oliver (DC).

     I have been in correspondance with a large family in common
descent from an Asa Croasmun, husband of Patience Oliver, born
in 1765, and buried at Cherry Tree. The parentage of this Asa
has been the quest of Dale Croasmun, Barbara Silveira, Marion
Croasmun, and Alfred M. Denman for many years. Dale, Barbara,
and Marion are now comfortable with claiming James-5 (#73) Croasman
as the father of Asa Croasmun of Cherry Tree. I am grateful to
Marion Croasmun for providing the information of most of Asa'a
descendants, and to Dale and Barbara for their deligent and
apparently successful search for the parentage of Asa Croasmun.
The following paragraphs are taken from a letter I received from
Dale Croasmun on December 24, 1982: (ROC)

     "My reasons for the ancestors of Asa and how I arrived at them
are as follows." (DC)

     "1- Barbara Silvera is a descendant of Joseph Croasman
who was the son of Asa. He went west very early and the records
she has indicate the correct spelling of the name as 'Croasmun'.
He was not in contact with the rest of the family so he must have
taken the spelling with him." (DC)

     "2- Asa's tombstone (and wife Patience Oliver) is spelled
'Croasmun'. Spent a lot of time finding it." (DC)

"3- Early land records are spelled Croasmun except for the family that went to Washington D.C." (DC)

"From the above I concluded Asa brought the spelling from New England, although it is spelled Crossman about as often as it is Croasmun. I then concentrated on the various towns in Mass. & New Hampshire and made four trips plus several to the Library of Congress. I went through all the record of the Old Colony Historical Society and have a brief case full of Crossmans. I visited Sutton, Easton, Boston, Middleboro, Charlton, Berlin, and of course Taunton & Rayham. In New Hampshire it was Masan (Manadnock - Marbboro) Concord & Hanover." (DC)

"My case is as follows:

"1- James was a transient (a house wright) and was warned from many of the about towns. He finally settled in Manadnock N.H. and thanks to a very accurate account of the town with no spelling corrections, was listed as James Croasman. This was in 1768." (DC)

"2- His son James Jr. listed as coming from Manadnock married Mary Priest in Haldeston. This same James was in the from Balton & Harwich and in the New Eng Gen Register Vol L. Pg 34 is in Col. Bigelow Buttall, Capt Barnes Company and spells his name CROSMUN jr. This same James applies for a pension and dates a transfer to Oswego, N.Y. to live with his son. His letter is signed CRAWSMAN which is approximately the way I pronounce CROASMUN." (DC)

"3- A Mercy Croasman 2nd married Wm Davenport in Narton in 1765 which is the earliest spelling I have. I have been unable to identify this Mercy and I do not know if she was Mercy the second or that was her second marriage." (DC)

"4- James Jr. has a daughter Eunice who married Geo. Conant and lived some 10 miles from Asa in Hanover." (DC)

"5- Elijah lived in Lyne, N.Y. 10 miles from Asa's Hanover and was listed in 1790 Census. Elijah was probably a son of James Jr. at least the ages fit." (DC)

"That is about it for the Asa - James Sr. relationship and if true, Asa would have been born in Charlton Mass in 1765 (James Sr was warned from the town). The reason Asa was not listed in the birth records of Charlton was that the New England towns did not list children of warned people for fear they would have to support them on their welfare rolls some day. Many were removed from the town and sent to the town of their origin. (Stephen and wife from Narton to Taunton for example)." (DC)

JAMES-5 (#73) CROASMAN/CROSSMAN continued from page

"Now to James Sr.

"Edgar Crossman's notes in the O.C. listed Joseph & Deborrah
had seven children. No. 6 was James who married Sarrah _____ in
1745 June 18. He also listed Mary Cary as his second wife which
was really Joseph III so that does not match. The James Sr. I
traced did marry Sarrah Ryfard in 1745/46 and had James II on
3/2/1746. I believe they had Asa in 1765." (DC)

"This is the only trace I have that James Sr was the same
James son of Joseph & Deborah born in 1721. I want to look
over Edgars notes again to make sure I have them right and to
look for another source. I hope to find it in Easton where
James was born and hopefully to find a Croasmun spelling there.
If it works out James father was Joseph who was son of Joseph
& Sarah Alden who was son of Robert." (DC)

"If you have anything that would support the above I would
appreciate it. Otherwise I'll go to New England in the Spring
and hopefully wrap it up. As you know Joseph was quite well
known in Easton and I believe I can trace it. I know where he
is burried but it is probably too much to expect the spelling
on his tombstone. Everyone wahted to 'correct' the spelling.
I even recommended to my son that he change it. I've since told
him to be proud of it...." Sincerely, Dale " (DC)

Genealogy of the Crossman Family, Supplement #3 • ©1990 by Robert Owen Crossman • 908 Front • Conway, AR 72032

The following seven pages are a chronology of James Crossman, son of Joseph and Deborah Pratt Crossman of Easton, Massachusetts as compiled by Dale F. Croasmun on July 1, 1988.

Dale F. Croasmun
July 1, 1988

1721   James Crossman, born 5th child – twin, at Easton, MA. (1)

1722   Mary Priest, born to Joseph and Mary Priest, Mar. 23, at Lancaster, MA. (2,3)

1744   Rebecca Proctor, born to Moses Proctor (later married James Crossman, Jr. (4)

1745   James Crossman, married Sarah Riford (Ryford). (5)

1745/6 James Crossman, Jr., born to James and Sarah Crossman. (5)

1748   Sarah, daughter, born to James and Sarah Crossman, Oct. 25. (5)

1760   Mary Crossman, of Dorchester, married Aaran Garfield of Shrewsbury, MA. Mary later became Molly and in old age, Moll, and was an alleged witch as per Shrewsbury History. Molly had children - Deborah 1761, Ruth___Daniel 1766. (6)

1762   Sarah Crossman, married Philip Clement, Jr., Charlton, Dec.3.

1763   James Crossman bought land from Aaron Garfield, Shrewsbury,MA.(1)

1765   James Crossman warned from Chrlton, MA. (1)

1765   James Crossman bought land from John Wood, Sept. 20, the John Wilson Tract, (Marlboro, NH). (7)

1765   Asa Croasmun, born somewhere. (8)

1768   James Crossman, sold Shrewsbury land (3 acres) to Aaron Garfield for three (3) pounds. (9)

1768   James Crossman, filed intention, on Aug. 20, to marry Mary Priest of Lancaster,listed as Junior (which the author believes was a mistake) and as coming from Manadnock, NH (Marlboro). (10).

---

(1)   Old Colony Records, by Edgar Crossman.
(2)   Lancaster, MA Records.
(3)   Priest Family History.
(4)   Mary Byron Family, Hollis History.
(5)   Dorchester,MA Vital Statistics.
(6)   Shrewsbury History.
(7)   Keene, NH Land Records.
(8)   Cemetery Stone, Cherry Tree, Indiana County, PA.
(9)   Worchester, MA Land Records.
(10) Lancaster, MA Vital Statistics.

1768   Mary Priest, intent, marriage, Aug. 20. (10)

1768   James (No Junior) and Mary Priest, Sept. 1, declare
        intention of marriage. (10)

1768   James (No Junior) and Mary Priest are married, Oct. 17, by
        Reverend Timothy Harrington. (10)

1769   Elijah Crossman, son, born to James and Mary Crossman,
        June 10, (son Johnathin name crossed off). (10)

1770   Croasman listed as seller in Manodnock, NH, and with a family
        on John Wilson Tract. (Note: He spelled his name
        Croasman.) (11)

1772   Eunice Crossman, daughter, born to James and Mary Crossman, at
        Bolton, MA. She later married George Conant and lived at
        Enfield, NH, ten miles from Hanover. George died fairly
        well to do in Enfield in 1838 and Eunice died in 1840.
        Buried in Enfield. b. Mar. 16, 1772, died May 2, 1840.

1773   James recorded land sale to Garfield at Shrewsbury. (6)

1775   James Crossman, Jr., Military Record Pension Application.
        Born at Roxbury, MA, 1746. Enlisted first, May 1, 1775
        for eight (8) months, living at Hardwick, MA. Enlisted
        at Bolton, MA in 1777. Marched to Saratoga, saw Burgoyne
        surrender. Transferred his pension to Palermo, Oswego
        County, NY, in 1835. Moved from Hardwick, MA to
        Lancaster, MA, then to Mason, NH, about 1787. He died
        either in Mason, NH, in 1836, or where he had transferred
        his pension, Palermo, NY. He spelled his name Crossmun on
        a Military Pension Application. There are many references
        to him at Mason, NH, in Town Records as being in care of
        the Town (before Pension). (12)

1779   James Crossman of Plainfield, NH, filed intention to marry
        Molly Smith. (13)

1787   James Crossman ("a transient person" and Rebecca Proctor of
        Hollis, NH, were married Feb.25, 1787 by Noah Womster,Esq.(14)

1788   James Crossman, on Jan. 21-24, 1788, who came from Plainfield,NH
        was warned from Hollis, NH. No family listed. On next line
        of record Rebecca Priest also warned. She came from Groton,
        County of Middlesex, NH. (She could have been a relative
        of Mary Priest, wife of James. (14)

---

(11)   Manodnock Proprieters Record.
(12)   Military Pension Application, Town Records, Mason, NH.
(13)   Norton, MA Vital Statistics.
(14)   Hollis, NH Town Records.

1788   James Crossman, (Jr.) on tax records of Mason, NH. (15)

1790   Elijah Crossman, at Lyme, NH, alone, 1790 Census. (16) Census,
        1790, James Crossman, at Mason, NH, with wife and son. (16)

1792   Elijah Crossman, of Lyme, NH, married Lydia Powers, of
        Groton, MA, Aug. 2. (17)

1792   Cloe born to Asa Crossman, Sept. 12, 1792. (18)

1794   Asa born to Asa Crossman, Oct. 15, 1794. (18)

1796   Rebecca born to Asa Crossman, Sept. 3, 1796. (18)

1798   Joseph born to Asa Crossman, Sept. 12, 1798. (18)

1800   Asa Crossman, with above noted family plus one son in
        Hanover, NH. (19)

1802   Mary (Priest) Crossman, of Plainfield, NH, (10 miles from
        Hanover) referred to in Town Records. "This may certify
        to all concerned that there now remains of the estate of
        Mary Crossman, late of Plainfield, deceased, who was in
        her last sickness under the care of the said town, the
        sum of eleven dollars - which sum is deposited in the
        Treasury of said Plainfield." Signed: Blass, Cody, Calley,
        Selectmen, Mar. 8, 1802, Steven G., Clerk. (20)

1804   Nathan Crossman, born in New York State, 1804. (21)

1810   Elijah Crossman at Hoosick Falls, NY. Son buried there. (22)

1810   Asa Crossman, Mahoning Township, Indiana County, PA, with
        3 male children under 10 (Oliver, Nathan, and William)
        2 male children, 10 - 16, (Asa and Joseph)
        1 male person, 26 - 45 (Asa Crossman, Sr.)
        2 females, 10 - 16 (Chloe and Rebecca)
        1 female, 26 - 45 (Patience). (22)

1820   Asa Crossman, Joseph Crossman, Asa Crossman, Jr., and
        John Piper and Benjamin Dykes listed as taxables in
        Perry Township, Jefferson County, PA. (23)

---

(15)   Mason, NH Tax Records.
(16)   1790 Census.
(17)   Reverend Page Records.
(18)   Hanover, NH Records.
(19)   1800 Census.
(20)   Plainfield, NH Town Records.
(21)   1850 Census.
(22)   1810 Census.
(23)   1820 Census.

Genealogy of the Crossman Family, Supplement #3 • ©1990 by Robert Owen Crossman • 906 Front Street • Conway, Arkansas 72032

From the previous records on James Crossman - Croasman, I have
deduced that he is the most likely candidate for the Father of
Asa Croasmun who settled at Georgetown, Punxsutawney, and Cherry Tree,
Pennsylvania and is buried near Cherry Tree having died there in 1828.

I would like to expand on the above facts to indicate why I
believe James was Asa's father and to lay a trail for future histor-
ians to examine to prove or disprove this relationship. I really
believe there is no birth certificate for Asa as I have visited the
logical areas for his birth and have never seen his name mentioned
until his children are listed at Hanover, New Hampshire, in 1798.
That does not mean that a birth certificate does not exist because
both New Hampshire and Massachusetts still have many unpublished
records.

As indicated in the chronology, James was the fifth child of
Joseph and Deborah Pratt Crossmun of Easton, Massachusetts. Joseph
was a respected member of the community, a church elder, treasurer
of the town, and one of its earliest settlers. He was the son of
Joseph and Sarah Alden Crossman and a grandson of Robert and
Sarah Kingsbury Crossman. He is buried at Easton alongside his son,
Joseph, who died the same year, 1777.

Little is known of James until he appears in the Dorchester
marriage record as marrying Sarah Riford or Ryford and in 1746 having
a son James. Edgar Crossman of Taunton, Massachusetts, who did a
great deal of work on the early Crossmans, indicated in some of his
correspondence that he believed this was the same James who was the
son of Joseph.

James and Sarah had another child in 1748. Then little is
known of him until 1763 when he bought land from Aaron Garfield at
Shrewsbury, Massachusetts. James was listed on the deed as a
housewright. From his travels and lack of substantial roots, I have
surmised that he was an itinerant carpenter who never really settled
down. Hence the lack of birth certificates for his children.

Three years earlier in 1760 a Mary Crossman married the same
Aaron Garfield. Aaron Garfield was born in 1736 and Mary would have
had to be a child of Sarah Riford and given the name Crossman after
Sarah Riford married James. I do not know of any other Crossman
families in the immediate area of Shrewsbury at that time. Sarah,
a known daughter of James and Sarah married Philip Clement, Jr.,
in Charlton, Massachusetts in 1762.

Shrewsbury and Charlton, Massachusetts are very close to each
other and James Crossman was warned from Charlton in 1765. Warning
a person from a New England town does not have any significant stigma,
but was more or less a legal maneuver to make sure the town would not

be responsible for the person in the event of illness, old age, or becoming destitute. The town where the person was born was responsible in all cases and all newcomers without jobs were warned including some visitors. That is one reason birth certificates for children were difficult to come by for transient people.

In 1765, the year Asa was born, James bought land from John Wood at a new settlement names Manadnock No. 5 in New Hampshire. This was a proprietorship settlement, meaning investors in Boston had bought the land and given or sold lots to settlers if they would make improvements. This town struggled to exist but finally became Marlboro, New Hampshire. James is listed as a settler in 1770 with his family. It is this record where James spelled his last name <u>Croasman</u> which I believe is the best piece of evidence that James really was the father of Asa.

James's wife, Sarah, must have died but there is no record of her death. In August, 1768, James filed intention to marry Mary Priest of Lancaster. This marriage intention lists James as Junior and coming from Manodnock. But there is another filing on October 17, 1768, and there is no mention of Junior. I believe the Junior was a mistake because Mary Priest was born to Joseph and Mary Priest on March 23, 1722, only one year after James, Senior, was born. It would appear that Asa had a stepmother at the age of three.

Mary Priest had two children to James: Elijah, born June 10, 1769, and Eunice, born March 16, 1772. There was one other child, Johnathin, a twin of Elijah but his name was crossed off the record. He probably died soon after birth. Mary was fifty years old at the time of this birth but Eunice survived to wed George Conant, the son of a storekeeper at Enfield, New Hampshire, and she is buried there having died in 1840. Enfield is about ten miles from Hanover, New Hampshire.

In 1770, James is listed as a settler in Manadnock but also sells his land the same year. He apparently was at Manodnock a very short time because Elijah was born at Lancaster, Massachusetts in 1769 and Eunice was born at Bolton, Massachusetts in 1772. He had not settled down but those two children did get registered. Bolton and Lancaster are not far from each other.

Quite a bit is known about James, Jr., from his military record and I believe he was at home, certainly unmarried at the time he enlisted at Bolton, so James, Senior, was near Bolton in 1777. Asa would have been twelve (12) when his older brother enlisted. James, Jr. also said he lived at Lancaster before moving to Mason, New Hampshire so James, Senior, and family probably lived there also.

The next record of a James comes from Norton, Massachusetts and a James Crossman files an intention to marry a Molly Smith in 1779. James is listed as from Plainfield, New Hampshire and I believe this is James, Jr., but his father is living at Plainfield, New Hampshire. This marriage apparently did not take place. James, Jr., did get married to Rebecca Proctor of Hollis, New Hampshire in 1787 and moved to Mason, New Hampshire and remained there until 1835. There are many records in that town concerning James and his wife.

In 1779 a James , who I believe was James, Senior, was warned from Hollis, New Hampshire, the same place as the original home of the wife of James, Jr., and he was listed as coming from Plainfield, New Hampshire. On the very next line of the town record, Rebecca Priest of Groton, Massachusetts was also warned from the town. Rebecca Priest could have been a relative of Mary Priest, wife of James, Senior.

In the 1790 Census only James, Jr., in Mason, New Hampshire, with a wife and son, Ickabod, and Elijah, the son of James and Mary were listed. Elijah was alone. In 1792 Elijah married Lydia Powers of Groton, Massachusetts, the same town as the above reference to Rebecca Priest.

In the same year, 1792, the birth certificates of four of Asa's children are listed with Chloe being the oldest. These children are all listed in one paragraph and were born in the period between 1792 and 1798. It does not list the fifth child of Asa and Patience (Oliver) but he is counted in the 1800 Census for Hanover, New Hampshire.

In 1802 a Mary Crossman of Plainfield, New Hampshire died and her $12 was deposited in the town treasury. I assume she was the wife of James and the former Mary Priest. At that time Asa was living in Hanover, New Hampshire. Elijah was living at Lyme, New Hampshire and Eunice was living at Enfield, New Hampshire. All these towns were established at about the same time and are all about ten (10) miles from Hanover. I believe James, Senior, had died and that they were one family.

About the same time, 1802 or 1803, Elijah moved to Hoosick Falls, New York, near Bennington, Vermont. And Asa started his trip to Pennsylvania. Nathan, his youngest son, was born in 1804 and listed his birthplace as New York in the 1850 Census. We could speculate that Elijah and Asa started west together and Elijah stopped at Hoosick Falls. Elijah's son, John, is buried at the North Hoosick Falls Cemetery. His name is spelled Crossman on the tombstone so Asa was the only one to keep the spelling Croasmun. James, Jr., in later military pension records did spell his name Crossmun but he also spelled it Crawsman at one time. His son, Ickabod, lived in Keene, New Hampshire and later moved to Palermo, New York and spelled his name Crossman.

        A Mercy Croasman (Crossman in the intention) married a
Benjamin Basset, Jr., in 1765 in Norton, Massachusetts. She
could have been a sister of Asa.

        From the above I believe Asa was the son of James and
Sarah Ryford Croasmun and was born in Manadnock No. 5, or
Marboro, New Hampshire, as it is now known. There was no town hall
and very few records except reports to the proprietors. No birth
certificates were recorded. Everything else fits as James travels
back and forth between Massachusetts and New Hampshire.

Dale F. Croasmun:bb
July 1, 1988

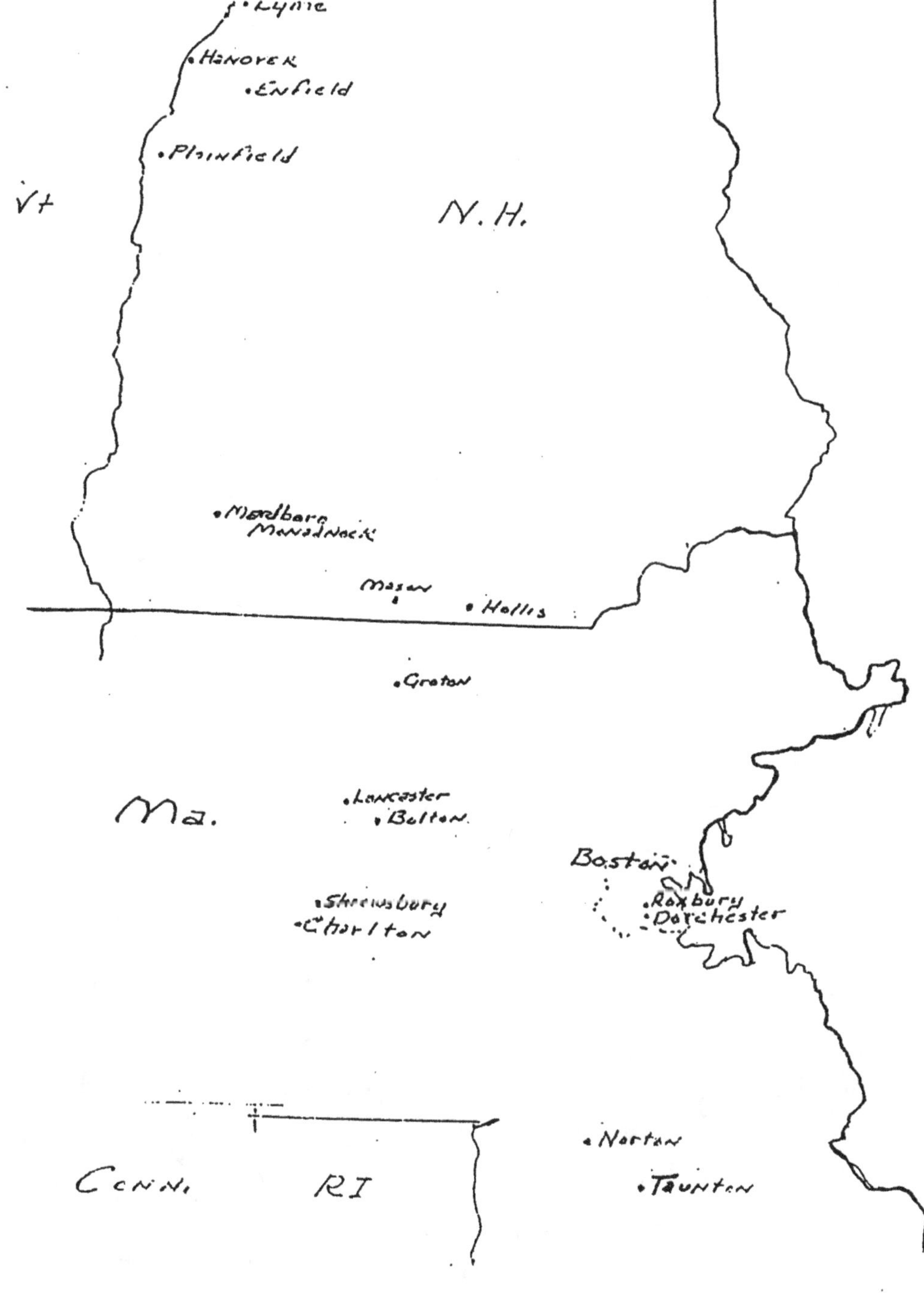

Our
Sixth
Generation

Page Number

Genealogy of the Crossman Family, Supplement #3 • ©1990 by Robert Owen Croasmun • 908 Front Street • Conway, Arkansas 72032

see page
485

ASA-6 CROSSMAN/CROASMUN (James-5, Joseph-4, Joseph-3,
                          Robert-2, John-1)

       b. 1765 (AD)
       d. May 29, 1828 at Cherry Tree, Indiana County, Penn.(AD)
       m.   1791 Patience Oliver at Rochester, Mass.(AD),
       Rochester, Mass. has no record of marriage (MC).

In The Boston Transcript of Oct. 3, 1910 it ask, "Can anyone
tell me who was Seth Crossman who married Patience Oliver of
Massachusetts about 1790?" So Asa might also have been known
as Seth. (BS)

       Children (Croasmun):

see page
494
CLOE-7 CROASMUN, b. 1792 at Cherry Tree, Indiana County,
       Pennsylvania (MC); or 1797 (MC);
       d.
       m.   1815 Benjamin Dight (MC)(AD), they had three
       children (AD).

see page
491
ASA-7 CROASMUN, JR., b.Oct. 15, 1794 in Massachusetts (AD)
            or in Cherry Tree, Indiana County, Penn.(MC);
       d.Feb. 19, 1864 (MC) in Pennsylvania (AD);
       m.July 15, 1819 Mary McHenry (MC), she was born Feb.
          12, 1799 (MC) and she died April 30, 1878 (MC) or
          1869 (AD). They had ten children (MC).

see page
492
REBECCA-7 CROASMUN, b.1796 in Mass.(AD) or April 9, 1795
            in Cherry Tree, Indiana County, Pennsylvania (MC);
       d.March 21, 1881 (MC) in Minnesota (AD);
       m.   1818 John Piper, he was born in 1799
          and died in 1857 (AD).
       They had eight children (AD). Ten children (MC).

see page
493
JOSEPH-7 CROASMUN, b. 1798 in Mass.(AD) or about 1797(MC);
            d. about 1837 (MC) in Pennsylvania (AD);
       m.Aug. 30, 1821 Catherine McHenry, she was born July
          21, 1796 (MC) and died in 1893 (AD), she later
          married John Alferd of Indiana Co., PA (MC).

OLIVER-7 CROASMUN, b. Aug. 16, 1800 (MC) in Mass.(AD)
            of Cherry Tree, Indiana County, Penn.(MC);
       d.Oct. 15, 1885 (MC) in Pennsylvania (AD);
       m.Aug. 30, 1821 Catherine Foster (MC) she was born
          Aug. 12, 1799 and died Nov. 2, 1830 (MC).
       m(2). June 9, 1835 Rachel O'Harrah (MC) or O'Hara (AD),
          she was born July 20, 1816 and died April 3, 1884(MC).
          He had five children by his first marriage and
          eight children by his second marriage (AD).

NATHAN-7 CROASMUN, b.1803 (AD)(MC);
       d.
       m.Hannah Branthoover or Brenthoover (MC);
          no children, they lived in Cherry Tree, Penn.(MC).

ASA-6 CROSSMAN/CROASMUN continued

Children continued:

WILLIAM-7 CROASMUN, b.1805 (AD)(MC);
     d. dissappeared in 1837 (MC);
     m.(1) 1829 Eva Hostler (AD), she died in 1835 (MC);
        Eva may have been second wife instead of first;
     m.(2) about 1836 Miss Wagner (AD).
        He had three children by his first marriage (AD).

Alfred M. Denman gives the following history of the OLIVER
family in a letter dated Sept. 4, 1977.
     ___________-1 Oliver, immigrant from England to Boston.
     ___________-2 Oliver, born in England or Boston.
     Peter-3 Oliver, b. 1670's near Boston, m. 1704 near
        Boston to Susanna Lisle, he died 1717 at Rochester,
        she died at Rochester, Mass. Had one son.
     Joseph-4 Oliver, b.Dec.12,1706 at Rochester; m.June 6,
        1734; d.Jan.5, 1790; m. to Ann Russell, she died at
        Rochester. Had five children.
     Joseph-5 Oliver, b.April 21, 1739 at Rochester; m. Nov.
        14, 1765 at Rochester to Dority Pettis; both died in
        Rochester. Had two daughters.
     Patience-6 Oliver, b. Nov. 18, 1766 at Rochester; m. ca
        1791 at Rochester to ASA CROSSMAN; both died at Cherry
        Tree, Pa. The marriage is surely proved by the five
        generations in Rochester. Reference given as'Rochester
        Town Records in Library.'
Alfred M. Denman gives the following history of Asa and
Patience Crossman in a letter dated Sept. 4, 1977.
'The trip out is somewhat conjecture. The marriage is
   surely proved by the 5 gens in Rochester. The trip out
   to Pennsylvania seems to have been taken by oxen and
   cart to start with and a study of (he typed off the page)..
   ..North West to the Hudson River which was crossed in
   about 1800 with 4 or 5 children, ages 8, 6, 4, and 2
   which made it really hard on the mother. Copy of a letter
   dated Aug. 22, 1977 from Marion Croasmun to me says -
   One 1880 Calwell History says he left N.E. in the early
   1800's and then later it shows him as a first settler of
   Cherry Tree in 1826. So it indicates that the younger
   children were born in N.Y. state. It so closely follows
   the trip written by me that I will give my interpretation
   of it.'
'The marriage of Asa and Patience was certianly in
Rochester as she was surely married at or near her home.
The start of the trip was surely by ox cart as they were
looking for a new home and may have started a new home
even in N.W. Mass., but went on across the Hudson River.
Somewhere I found the statement that they had stopped
for several years at least twice for supplies at least,
and finally the cart getting too small and the oxen too
small also, they stopped until the money for this could
be earned. Someway they used up the years until about

Asa-6 CROSSMAN/CROASMUN continued from page 6-2-a.

1812 when they finally came to Hamilton where they
started a farm and lived 6 or 8 years. During this
time in 1818 their daughter Rebecca married to John
Piper Jr., at this same place. This carried them to
1818 or 1820. This is as near as I can fill in the
years.'
'John PIPER was a lone son of ELLEN SMITH-PIPER who
became a widow in 1800 and soon married a widower named
Samuel Foster. Have never added anything to this SMITH
family in all the years I have worked on it. Daughter
ELLEN was captured by the Indians in 1789 near Fort
Ligonier and rescued 8 years later. She was a captive
across the River in Ohio from Pittsburg and there was no
travel here until after 1800.'
'ASA and PATIENCE Trip con. -- Letter dated Feb. 16,
1965 from EARL CROASMUN, quote - Our family record
show that ASA and PATIENCE were both born in 1765 near
Boston. One son William stayed on old farm near Hamilton.
He was born in 1805 so the move to Cherry Tree had to
be made 1825 to 8, or 30.'
"Asa was the only Crossman that was on the spot at the
right time. Much more probable." (AD)

Asa's son, William is reported to have been robbed and
murdered on a lumber trip to Maryland. (MC).

Inscription on Asa'a tombstone at Cherry Tree reads,
"Yes again we hope to meet thee when the day of life is
fled. Then in heaven with joy to greet thee, where no
farewell tears are shed." (MC).

Page 417 - History of Indiana County, PA., "The first
settlers in the vicinity of 'the Cherry Tree' were John
Bartlebaugh and Peter Gordon, the hunter, on the Clearfield
side in 1822. Asa Croasmun, William Sebring in the spring
of 1826." (MC)

Our
Seventh
Generation

Genealogy of the Crossman Family, Supplement #5 • ©1990 by Robert Owen Crossman • 908 Front Street • Conway, Arkansas 72032

ASA-7 CROASMUN   (Asa-6, James-5, Joseph-4, Joseph-3,
                         Robert-2, John-1)

    b. Oct. 15, 1794 in Massachusetts (AD) or in Cherry Tree,
       Indiana County, Pennsylvania (MC);
    d. Feb. 19, 1864 (MC) in Pennsylvania (AD);
    m. July 15, 1819 Mary McHenry (MC), she was born Feb. 12,
       1799 (MC) and she died April 30, 1878 (MC) or 1869(AD).
       They had eight children (AD).

        Children:

    CHILD-8 CROASMUN, b. a boy (MC);
            d. in infancy (MC).; buried on P.A. Weaver farm,
                formerly the William Drummond farm. (MC).
    CHILD-8 CROASMUN, b. a girl (MC);
            d. in infancy (MC); buried on P.A. Weaver farm (MC).

see page
502
    MARY-8 CROASMUN, b. Feb. 22, 1822 (MC);
            d.March 27,1905 (MC);
            m.(1)   Washington Crissman (MC);
            m.(2)   John William Barrack (MC);
            m.(3)   Irvin Robinson (MC).

see page
503
    ISAAC-8 CROASMUN, b.March 8, 1824 (MC);
            d.July 8, 1900 (MC);
            m.(1)   1846 Mary Ann Mutersbaugh, she was
                born Sept. 13, 1828 and died Feb. 25, 1864 (MC);
            m.(2) May 24, 1866 Elizabeth Peffer, she was b.April
                10,1835 and died Aug.13, 1890 (MC).
see page
505
    NATHAN-8 CROASMUN, b.April 9, 1826 (MC);
            d.Aug. 24, 1908 (MC);
            m.June 17, 1852 Rachel Mary Deniston Blose, she was b.
            March   9, 1829 and died Dec. 10, 1913 (MC).

see page
506
    ASA-8 CROASMUN, b.Oct. 1, 1828 (MC);
            d.July 12, 1906 (MC);
            m.Sept. 25, 1851 Mary Robinson, she was born April
                27, 1835 and died July 5, 1907 (MC).

see page
507
    MILES-8 CROASMUN, b.Sept. 10, 1831 (MC);
            d.Sept. 12, 1917 (MC);
            m.Jan. 5, 1871 Margaret Beck, she was born July 23,
                1844 and died March 31, 1939 (MC).

see page
508
    JAMES-8 CROASMUN, b.Nov. 9, 1834 (MC);
            d.March 26, 1911 (MC);
            m.   1857 Julia Ann Sutter, she was born
                Aug. 5, 1842 and she died July 26, 1916 (MC).

    WILLIAM-8 CROASMUN, b.Aug.25, 1836 (MC);
            d.Jan.25, 1853 aged 17yrs 4mo 25 days (MC).;
                "Saved by Grace" (MC).
see page
509
    ELIZABETH JANE-8 CROASMUN, b.April 25, 1842 (MC);
            d.April 23, 1902 (MC);
            m.   James Madison Chambers, he was born Dec.
                23, 1844 and died June 17, 1915 (MC).

REBECCA-7 CROSSMAN   (Asa-6, James-5, Joseph-4, Joseph-3,
                          Robert-2, John-1)

    b. Sept. 4, 1795 in Cherry Tree, Indiana County, Penn.(MC),
       or 1796 in Mass.(AD);
    d. March 21, 1881 (MC) in Minnesota (AD);
    m.   1818 John Piper, he was born in 1799 and died
       in 1857, he was born near Horatio or Hamilton, PA, son
       of John Piper and Ellen Smith Piper who were married
       in 1798 near the same place.(AD) He died March 21,1857 (MC).

    CHILDREN:

    ANN-8 PIPER, b.1819 near Horatio. (AD).
        d. 1902 near Mead, Washington (AD).
        m. 1841 in Allegheny County to Samuel Haldeman, he was
           born in 1815 and died in 1883 (AD). Had 5 children(AD).

    SARAH ELIZABETH-8 PIPER, b. 1821 in Horatio (AD);
        d. in MeLeod County, Minnesota (AD);
        m. 1840 in Jeff. Co., James Postlewaite, he was born in
           1809 and died in 1881 in MeLeod Co., Minn. They
           had 6 children (AD).

    REBECCA-8 PIPER, b.1822 in Horatio (AD);
        d. 1912 in Hamilton, Pa. (AD);
        m. 1844 in Jeff. Co., Winni Fred S. Neale. Had 6 children;
        m(2). Clark Cathcart. Had one child (AD).

    ELLEN-8 PIPER, b. 1825 in Horatio (AD);
        d.
        m. 1842 in Jeff. Co., John Packer, he was born in 1822
           and he died in 1868. They had 8 children (AD).

    JAMES ANTONY-8 PIPER, b. 1831 in Horatio (AD);
        d.
        m. 1853 to Lucinda Johnston, she was born in 1832 and
           she died in 1912. They had two children. (AD).

    NANCY KATH.-8 PIPER, b. 1834 in Horatio (AD);
        m. 1855 to Robert Callihan. They had 8 children (AD).

see page
501
WILLIAM ENOS-8 PIPER, b. 1837 in Horatio (AD);
        d. 1928 (AD);
        m. 1858 in Forest Co.?, to Sarah Ellen Mayze (or Mayse),
           she was born in 1843 and died in 1933 (AD). They
           had ten children (AD).

    SARAH JANE-8 PIPER, b. 1842 in Horatio (AD);
        d.
        m. 1863 in McLeod Co., Minnesota. No Children (AD).

This Piper allied family matted a barge, floated down the
Clarion river and Allegheny Rivers into the Ohio River,
landed and traded for oxen and covered wagons and went
across country to McLeod Co., Minn., all in the year 1859.
The grandmother Rebecca Crossman Piper accompanied them and
took a land claim near her sons and died there. They had
moved from southern Jeff. Co. to Clarion Co. in 1845. (AD)

JOSEPH-7 CROASMAN   (Asa-6, James-5, Joseph-4, Joseph-3,
                         Robert-2, John-1)

    b.   1798 in Massachusetts (AD) or about 1797(MC);
    d.   about 1837 (MC) in Pennsylvania (AD);
    m. Aug. 30, 1821 Catherine McHenry, she was born July
    21, 1796 (MC) and died in 1893 (AD). They had seven
    children (AD). Sometimes spelled name CROASMAN.

        Children: Croasman/   /Crossman
                 (not necessarily in order of birth)
    ASA-8 CROASMAN, b.1827 (BS);
             d.   1892 (MC);
         m. Mary Young, she was born in 1831 and d.1919(MC).

    OLIVER-8 CROASMAN, b.
             d. drowned at age 12 in Susquehanna River near
                 Burnside, PA (MC).
see page
496 MARY JANE-8 CROASMAN, b.Feb.20,1821 at Buena Vista,Bell TWP,
             Clearfield County, Pennsylvania (MC)
             d.March 14?, 1926 near Middletown, Oregon;
             m.   1841 Elias Brickley in Penn.
             See obituary on page 8-1.

see page
498 JAMES-8 CROASMAN, b.June 28, 1822 in Clearfield, PA(MC);
             d.June 4,1913 near Calistoga, California;
             m.(1) Levina Brinkley (BS)
             m.(2) Augusta Dielemann on Mar.10,1859, she was b.
                 Aug. 27, 1838 (MC). or TIELEMAN?
    REBECCA-8 CROASMAN, b.
             d.
             m. James Lewis (BS); in Indiana, PA (MC).

    CATHERINE-8 CROASMAN, b.
             d.
             m. Warren Clawson (BS).

    ELISA B.-8 CROASMAN, b.
             d.
             m. Cornelius Drake (MC).

CLOE-7 CROASMUN (Asa-6, James-5, Joseph-4, Joseph-3,
                        Robert-2, John-1)

b. 1792 or 1797 at Cherry Tree, Indiana County, PA(MC);
d.
m.   1815 Benjamin Dight (MC)(AD), he was a
   Presbyterian minister located in the Freeport,PA area(MC).

   CHILDREN:

ASA-8 DIGHT, b.   (MC)
   d.

MARIA-8 DIGHT, b.   (MC)
   d.

ROBERT-8 DIGHT, b.   (MC)
   d.

**This page is intentionally blank
to allow the next generation
to begin on a right hand page.**

Our
Eighth
Generation

Page Number

see page
493

MARY JANE-8 CROASMAN,   (Joseph-7, Asa-6, James-5, Joseph-4, Joseph-3,
                                            Robert-2, John-1)

    b. Feb. 20, 1821 at Buena Vista, Clearfield County, Penn;
    d. March 14?, 1926 near Middletown, Oregon;
    m.   1841 Elias Brickley in Pennsylvania.

The following obituary was sent to me by Barbara Silveira
of Oakland, California on September 24, 1976. It is taken
from the "Oregonian" March 17, 1926.

"Woman, aged 105, Dies. Mary Jane Brickley born in 1821.
200 Direct Descendants Survive Late Resident of District Near
Middletown, Oregon.
Mary Jane Brickley, one of the oldest residents of Oregon,
died Sunday at the home of her daughter, Mrs. E.E. Pointer,
near Middletown, Oregon, at the age of 105 years.
Mrs. Brickley was the daughter of Mr. and Mrs. Joseph Croasman
and was born at Buena Vista, Clearfield County, Pennsylvania,
February 20, 1821. She was married to Elias Brickley in
Pennsylvania in 1841. She left Pennsylvania in 1885, going
to Anita, Case county Iowa, where she lived for 5 years. The
Brickleys came to Oregon from Iowa in 1890 and settled first
at Hillsboro. Later they moved to Montana and then returned
to Oregon in 1910 and settled at Middletown.
13 children, 12 of whom are still living, were born to Mr.
and Mrs. Brickley, and altogether Mrs. Brickley is survived
by more than 200 direct descendants, including children,
grandchildren, grt.-grandchildren and great-great-grandchildren.
Her youngest child, Mrs. E.E. Pointer of Middletown, is 62
years old and the oldest, Mrs. Elizabeth Young of Iowa, is
past 84.
Mrs. Brickley was the third child in a family of 6, having
3 sisters and 2 brothers, all of whom preceded her in death.
One of her brothers, Rev. James Croasman, who was one of
the first preachers in Oregon, died about 1920 at the age
of 92. He was a pastor of the First Evangelical church at
Salem.
The 12 living children of Mrs. Brickley are A.W. Brickley of
Portland, Joseph Brickley of Middletown, John Brickley of
Montana, E.E. Brickley of Pennsylvania, James C. Brickley of
Middletown, Francis Brickley of Pennsylvania, Mrs. E.E.
Pointer of Middletown, Mrs. Emma Heath of Portland, Mrs.
Elizabeth Young of Iowa, Mrs. Lavina Sebring, Mrs. Margaret
Stiffler and Mrs. Nora Anderson, all of Pennsylvania.
Funeral services were conducted yesterday from the Middletown
Friends church, Rev. C.I. Whitlock of Newberg officiating.
Internment was in the Middletown cemetary."

        Children (Brickley):

    ELIZABETH-9 BRICKLEY, b. before 1842; m.J.C.Young, of Iowa,
                                        he was b.1839(MC).
    A.W.-9 BRICKLEY, of Portland.

    JOSEPH-9 BRICKLEY, of Middletown.

    JOHN-9 BRICKLEY, of Montana.

    ELMER E.-9 BRICKLEY, of Harrisburg, Pennsylvania (MC).

see page
496

MARY JANE-8 CROSSMAN continued.

Children continued:

JAMES C.-9 BRICKLEY, of Middletown.

FRANCIS MARION-9 BRICKLEY, of Pennsylvania. (MC).

EMMA-9 BRICKLEY, m. W.M. Heath, of Portland (MC).

LAVINA-9 BRICKLEY, m. Ab. Sebring, of Pennsylvania (MC).

MARGARET-9 BRICKLEY, m. George Slawson (MC).

NORA-9 BRICKLEY, m. J. M. Anderson, of Penn. (MC).

CHRISTINE "Crissie"-9 BRICKLEY, b. 1884 (MC);
    d.March 18, 1964 (MC);
    m.   Elmer E. Pointer, he died Dec. 12,
      1927, buried in Middletown, Oregon cemetery(MC).
      Christine had a daughter, Mrs. Irene M. Dewey of
      R.D.#3 Box 246 Sherwood, Oregon 97140 (MC).

JAMES-8 CROASMAN, (Joseph-7, Asa-6, James-5, Joseph-4, Joseph-3,
                                    Robert-2, John-1)

    b.June 28, 1822 in Pennsylvania;
    d.June 4, 1913 near Calistoga, California;
    m.(1)   Levina Brinkley (BS);
    m.(2) MARCH 10,1859   Augusta Tielemann.(BS)

    The following memoir was sent to me by Barbara Silveira on
September 24, 1976. It was taken from the Journal of the 61st
Session of the California Conference held on September 17, 1913.
    "The Rev. James Croasman was a native of Pennsylvania, born
6/28/1822. He died near Calistoga, California, 6/4/1913.
Lacking 24 days, he was 91 years old. He was feeble only in
body. It was the physical that was old and weary and ready
to die. The mental man was remarkably alert. The spiritual
man was fully alive. He was young of heart and very compan-
ionable.
    Mr. Croasman's parents were pioneer Pennsylvania Methodists-
God fearing people, teaching their children reverence for the
Almighty, the Bible and the Sabbath, while they looked for
their conversion. To James this experience came when he was
22 years old at a camp meeting. Four years later (1848) he
joined the Pittsburg Conference of the Evangelical Association
in whose ministry he remained 37 years.
    In his boyhood there was no public school system, and his
educational advantages were limited to some private instruc-
tion in the elementary English branches. But he met with
credit the requirements of his Conference examinations, and
received his Orders at the regular time.
    James Croasman was truly a ministerial frontiersman,
evangelically blazing the way. He was successful too in
building churches, bringing people to Christ and gathering
them into the Household of Faith. God built him with a strong
frame and a rugged constitution in which was set an indomitable
will with a stout heart to do hard and brave things on large
circuits; and these printed lines are a poor summary of really
worthy achievements in spiritual things wrought in a humble
way for the Kingdom of Christ.
    From 1848 to 1863 he preached in Pennsylvania and Ohio, and
was called "The Peter Cartwright of the Evangelical Association."
They were vigorous, fruitful years, richly blessed of God.
Salaries were small, but the souls of men were precious, and
Christ and His Church were honored in cheerful sacrifice.
    In 1863 he was sent to Oregon where he built churches and
held successful revivals. Salem and Corvallis were his appoint-
ments. Among the converts at Salem was John H. Bates, whom
he licensed to preach, and who is now a Methodist Episcopal
minister and author of a volume - "Christian Science and Its
Problems." At Corvallis he held a public debate with a
"Cambellite" preacher who had openly denied the work of the
Holy Spirit in conversion. Mr. Croasman then followed the
debate with a protracted meeting in which fully a hundred
people were converted, witnessing to the inward testimony of
the Holy Spirit.   498

see page
498

JAMES-8 CROASMAN continued.

In 1869 he returned to the Pittsburg Conference, preaching
in the oil regions, establishing an English Mission and
building a church in Pittsburg, and doing similar successful
work in the Iowa Conference until 1875 when he came back to
Oregon, to Corvallis, Independence, Salem, and Dayton. From
1882 to 1885 he was in charge at Sacramento, California and
built the Evangelical Association Church on K Street.
In 1885 he became a Supply in the Nevada Mission of our
Church under Superintendent George W. LaMatyr. On the
recommendation of the Mission, the California Conference in
1887 received him into its membership on his Credentials.
His work with us was wholly in the Nevada Mission at the
following places: Mason Valley, Indian Valley, Loyalton and
Genoa. In Mason Valley the saloon-keepers and their supporters
bitterly opposed the Church, and peripatetic evangelists
teaching false doctrines were another set of disturbers cal-
ling out the fighting qualities of the old circuit-rider
whose rich experience, soundness of doctrine and skill in
defense were more than equal to all opposition. On his way
to Indian Valley he was kicked by a horse and lay for weeks
unconscious, while his life was despaired of. The years work
was thereby seriously crippled. On the Loyalton Circuit he
had a gracious revival, though the Congregationalist gathered
most of the fruit. From Genoa he retired, having given in
all 42 years of very effective service. The years since
1890 have been spent mostly in Sacramento, Santa Cruz, and
Berkeley, where he and his wife have been beloved by enlarging
circles of friends.
His reception by our Conference, when he was 65 years old,
was unusual, but he has been nought save a blessing to our
Church. He belonged to that class of courageous men who
conquer wildernesses, whose work in wrought in kingdoms
more enduring than those of finance and statecraft. He left
no money fortune behind. But his record of service for
the church and humanity is stamped with the seal of Divine
approval as it has been attended with God's blessing. He and
his work will be honored in the Last Great Day. His life,
character and ministry make the precious, priceless legacy
his beloved wife and devoted children inherit from a noble
husband and father who is now entered into the fellowship
of the Company within the Veil. James H.N.Williams."

JAMES-8 CROASMAN continued.

CHILDREN (by first wife):

ALLEN BOOKHIMER-9 CROASMAN, b.June 7,1846 (MC);
    d.Sept.3,1935 (BS);   *CHILDREN OF ALLEN & LINNIE*
    m.Linnie McCully (MC).   *ALICE -10 BOOKHIMER, M. DUSTIN (BS)*
                                    LILLIAN-10 BOOKHIMER, M. CHARLES SINCLAIR (

CHILDREN (by second wife):

SEE PAGE 511 OREGON ELLSWORTH-9 CROASMAN, b.Jan.11,1865 in Oregon (BS);
    d. *JUNE 13, 1935 (BS)*
    m.Jan.18,1900 Helen Gay King (MC).

MARTIN-9 CROASMAN, b.Aug.27,1866 (MC);
    d. young and left no descendants (BS).
        MURDERED BY NEIGHBOR WHEN TEENAGER (BS)
FRANK-9 CROASMAN, b. Oct.28,1875 (BS);
    d. *AUG. 1, 1950 (BS) M(1) EFFIE ___ (BS); M(2) CLARA ___ (BS)*
    He left no descendants (BS).

LINNIE AUGUSTA-9 CROASMAN, b. May 3, 1878 (BS);
    d.   1968 (MC);
    m. ~~she left no descendants (BS)~~.
        M(1) WILLIAM BARTELS (BS)
        M(2) ___ BETTENHOUSE (BS)
        CHILDREN (OF LINNIE & WILLIAM)
            TWIN -10 BARTELS; DIED AT BIRTH (BS)
            TWIN -10 BARTELS; DIED AT BIRTH (BS)
            DOROTHY-10 BARTELS, B
                B. MAY 18, 1905
                D. JAN. 2, 1983
            DIXIE -10 BARTELS, DIED AT BIRTH (BS)

THIS INFORMATION WAS PROVIDED BY BARBARA SILVEIRA ON OCT. 13, 1977

THIS PAGE NOT FULLY INDEXED.

see page
492

WILLIAM ENOS-8 PIPER (Rebecca-7, Asa-6, James-5, Joseph-4, Joseph-3,
Robert-2, John-1)

b. Oct. 6, 1837 Jefferson County, Horatio, Pennsylvania(AD);
d. Sept.18,1928 Spokane, Washington, buried in Pleasant
    Praire Cemetery, Spokane Washington.
m. Feb. 15,1858 Sarah Ellen Mayze, dau. of William Mayze
    and Sophia Herring Mayze, she was born Feb.22,1843 at
    Marionville, Forest Co., Penn., and she died Aug. 13,
    1933 at Spokane, Washington (AD).

CHILDREN:

SARAH KATHARINE-9 PIPER, b.March 30,1859 at Marionville,PA(AD);
    d. 1865 in Minnesota (AD).

ALVERETTA-9 PIPER, b.April   1862 in Lester Praire,Minn.(AD);
    d. 1864 in Minnesota (AD).

see page
510
ESTHER OLIVE-9 PIPER,b.May 31,1864 Lester McLeod, Minnesota(AD);
    d.Aug.12,1942 at Spokane,Washington (AD);
    m. 1884 Monroe Denman, he was born 1858 and died 1932(AD).

LAVILIA HOLMES-9 PIPER,b.Nov.16,1866 Lester,Minnesota(AD);
    d.Jan.21,1958 (AD).

EVA ADELINE-9 PIPER,b.March 3, 1869 Lester,Minnesota (AD);
    d. 1954 (AD);
    m. 1943 Jack Spoar in Spokane County, Washington (AD).

WILLIAM OSCAR-9 PIPER, b.Feb.8,1871 Lester,Minnesota(AD);
    d.May 5, 1957 (AD); unmarried (AD).

JAMES ANTHONY-9 PIPER, b.May 8,1874 Lester,Minn.(AD);
    d.Sept. 27,1958 (AD);
    m.Feb.15,1895 Bertha Worth in Minn. (AD); 8 children (AD).

ALBERT HERRON-9 PIPER, b.July 31,1876 Lester,Minn.(AD);
    d. Sept.19,1958 (AD);
    m. 1900 Clara Niccum in Minnesota (AD); one son (AD).

LUELLE MAYZE-9 PIPER, b.Jan.30,1879 Lester,Minn.(AD);
    d.May 4, 1974 (AD);
    m.1908 Winnifred Seth in Minnesota (AD);
    m.(2) 1931 Dr. W.D. Valentine in Spokane, Washington (AD).

HEBER BENNION-9 PIPER, b.July 8, 1883 Lester,Minn.(AD);
    d.April 22, 1934 (AD); unmarried (AD).

William and Sarah moved to Lester Praire, Minnesota in 1859
via canal boat and oxen team. He is a veteran of Company H,
2nd Regiment, Minnesota Volunteer Inf. They moved to Spokane,
Washington in 1894. Both are buried in Orchard Praire
Cemetery, Spokane County, Washington. Sarah Mayze's parents
married in 1837 in Penn., and had three children: James in
1839; Stephen in 1841; and Sarah Ellen in 1843. (AD)

MARY-8 CROASMUN   (Asa-7, Asa-6, James-5, Joseph-4, Joseph-3,
                                  Robert-2, John-1)

    b. Feb. 11 or 22, 1822 (MC);
    d. March 27, 1905 (MC);
    m.(1)   Washington Crissman (MC);
    m.(2)   John William Barrack (MC);
    m.(3)   Irvin Robinson (MC).

        CHILDREN:

see page
512 MARY ELIZA-9 CRISSMAN, b.
        d.
        m.   Michael Lantz (MC).

see page
513 ELIZABETH ANN-9 BARRACK, b.May 26, 1853 (MC);
        d. Feb. 6, 1924 (MC);
        m. Dec. 28, 1877 or 1876 Abram Hicks, he was born
            July 15, 1852 and died Nov. 29, 1920 (MC).

see page
514 MATILDA JANE "Jennie"-9 ROBINSON, b.Jan.17,1857 (MC);
        d. Aug. 19, 1929 (MC);
        m. March 12, 1874 Michael Harwick (or Harwig), he was
            born Dec. 29, 1854 and died Oct. 1940 (MC).

see page
491

ISAAC-8 CROSSMAN (Asa-7,Asa-6, James-5, Joseph-4, Joseph-3,
                                  Robert-2, John-1)
b. March 8, 1824 (MC);
d. July 8,1900, buried at Oakwood Cemetery, Falls Church,VA(MC);
m.(1)   1846 Mary Ann Mutersbaugh, she was born Sept.13,
     1828 and died Feb.25,1864, she is buried in White Church-
     yard, Hamilton, Pennsylvania (MC);
m.(2)May 24,1866 Elizabeth M. Peffer, she was born April 10,
     1835 and died Aug. 13, 1890 (MC).
Isaac, unlike his father, spelled his name Crossman.
     CHILDREN:

see page
515

EVALINE-9 CROSSMAN, b.Sept.8,1847 (MC);
     d.Aug.11,1874 (MC);
     m.Nov. 1867 William E. Vandermark (MC).

JOHN MILTON-9 CROSSMAN, b.Sept.2,1849 (MC);
     d.Aug.17,1933 (MC);
     m.Nov. 1877 Anna Maria Forbes, she was b.March 25,1847 and
        she died April 5, 1930 (MC).
        CHILDREN:
           NELLIE MARIA-10 CROSSMAN, b.April 10,1879 (MC);
              d.Aug.28,1927 (MC); unmarried (MC).
           FRANCES FORBES "Fannie"-10 CROSSMAN, b.Feb.12,1883(MC);
              d.May 30,1954 (MC); unmarried (MC).
           BESSIE W.-10 CROSSMAN, b.Sept.24,1885 (MC); m. Blake
              Palm, now divorced, they had no children (MC).
           EFFIE MAY-10 CROSSMAN, b.Aug.22,1886 (MC); d.Nov.1886
              died at 3 months of age (MC).

JAMES McHENRY-9 CROSSMAN, b.Feb.10,1852 (MC);
     d.Aug.13,1932 (MC);
     m.April 1900 Maggie Keeler Birch Brown, she was b.1851(MC);
        she died May 14,1930 (MC); no children (MC).

MARILLA JANE-9 CROSSMAN, b.July 17, 1854 (MC); an artist (MC);
     d.May 22, 1899 (MC) in Chattanooga, Tenn., unmarried(MC).

DAVID CLARK-9 CROSSMAN, b.Dec.1,1856 (MC);
     d.Oct.19,1885 unmarried (MC).

FLORA BELLE-9 CROSSMAN, b.Aug.13,1859 (MC);
     d.Sept.11,1956 (MC);
     m.Dec.14,1882 Frank Lest Birch, he was b.May 25,1858 and
        d. June 26,1939 (MC).
        CHILDREN:
           ESSIE FLORENCE-10 BIRCH, b.July 4,1884 and d.Dec.14,
              1967 unmarried (MC).
           MARY NEDETTA-10 BIRCH, b.Oct.3,1888 and d. April 23,
              1957 unmarried (MC).
           ISAAC FRANKLIN-10 BIRCH, b.Oct.8,1890 and d.April 8,
              1940 (MC); m.Nov.11,1922 Elsie Wright, she was b.
              March 8,1901, no children (MC).
           MILTON TAYLOR-10 BIRCH, b.Dec.8,1895 (MC); m.Pauline
              Waite (MC); no children (MC).

continued

ISAAC-8 CROSSMAN continued

CHILDREN continued:

see page
516 GEORGE GRANT-9 CROSSMAN, b.Feb.9 or 24,1862 (MC);
    d.Jan.24,1941 (MC);
    m.April 7,1892 Mary Ellen "Nellie" M Dodge, she was
        born March 25,1871 and died March 23,1951 (MC).

ISAAC MUTERSBAUGH-9 CROSSMAN, b.Feb.18,1864 (MC);
    d.March 15, 1864 aged one month (MC).

CHILDREN (of second marriage):

MARY ELIZABETH-9 CROSSMAN, b.Feb.28,1870 (MC);
    d.Jan.14,1958 (MC); no children(MC);
    m.Dec.14,1898 John William Mutersbaugh, he was born
        April 17,1865 and died June 27,1930(MC), he was the son
        of Rev. David Mutersbaugh and Ellen Louise Appleby
        Mutersbaugh, Rev. David was the nephew of Mary Ann
        Mutersbaugh, Isaac's first wife.(MC).

SUSIE ANN-9 CROSSMAN, b.July 17,1873 (MC);
    d.June 13,1968 (MC); unmarried (MC).

CHARLES ISAAC-9 CROSSMAN, b. Jan.1,1879 (MC);
    d.Jan.1,1922 (MC);
    m.Oct.5,1905 Pansy Payne, she was born Jan.21,1881(MC).
        CHILDREN:
            CLARK-10 CROSSMAN, b. Sept. 2, 1902 (MC);
                m. Mrs. Betty Wilson, she was born Aug.4,1896(MC).

****

see page
491

NATHAN-8 CROASMUN (Asa-7,Asa-6, James-5, Joseph-4, Joseph-3,
                                  Robert-2, John-1)
   b. April 9, 1826 (MC);
   d. Aug. 24, 1908 (MC); buried in White Churchyard, Hamilton,PA.
   m. June 17, 1852 Rachel Mary Deniston Blose, she was born
       March 9, 1829 and died Dec. 10, 1913 (MC), she was the
       daughter of George Blose and Esther Ament Blose (MC).
   m.(2) Jan.2,1906 Ruth Lyons, b.Dec.2,1862 and d.Nov.11,1925(MC).
       CHILDREN:

CYRUS GEORGE-9 CROASMUN, b.March 27,1853 (MC);
    d.Aug.29,1855 age 2 years 5 months 2 days (MC), buried in
       White Churchyard, Hamilton, Penn. (MC).

see page
517

WILLIAM ASA-9 CROASMUN, b.Aug.8,1855 (MC);
    d.June 18,1923 (MC); buried in White Churchyard (MC).
    m.Sept.30,1885 Sarah Rebecca Elizabeth Neal, she was b.
       Feb.19,1861 and died Jan.17,1938 (MC).

see page
518

JOHN DARWIN-9 CROASMUN, b.April 23,1858 (MC);
    d.Feb.11,1933 (MC); buried White Churchyard,Hamilton,PA(MC);
    m.June 19,1887 Anna May Coulter, she was b. May 1,1864 and
       died May 27,1927 (MC).

IOLA JANE-9 CROASMUN, b. Aug. 17,1860 (MC);
    d.April 10,1936 (MC); unmarried (MC); buried at Hamilton,PA.

see page
519

INA MAUD-9 CROASMUN, b.Oct.12,1863 (MC);
    d.Oct.24,1934 (MC); buried at Barrets Chapel, Delaware(MC).
    m.Sept.2,1891 Howard Bruce Defibaugh, he was born Sept. 17,
       1864 and died Nov.17,1927 (MC).

see page
520

DARIUS MILES "Dess"-9 CROASMUN, b.June 20,1866 (MC);
    d.Jan.3,1943 (MC);
    m. Dec.26,1889 Miranda McHenry, she was born Dec.6,1867
       and died Sept.23,1897(MC).

        CHILDREN (of second marriage):

SILAS RALPH-9 CROASMUN, b. Oct.17,1869 (MC);
    d. May 28,1916 (MC);
    m. July 14,1915 Jeannette M. Ittel (MC).

****

ASA-8 CROASMUN (Asa-7, Asa-6, James-5, Joseph-4, Joseph-3,
                                 Robert-2, John-1)

b. Oct. 1, 1828 (MC);
d. July 12, 1906 (MC); both buried at White Cem.,Hamilton,PA.
m. Sept. 24, 1851 Mary Robinson, she was born April 27,
   1830 and died July 5, 1907 (MC).

CHILDREN:

see page
521 HENRIETTA MARIA-9 CROASMUN, b. July 4, 1852 (MC);
    d. March 12, 1932 (MC);
    m. Nov. 27, 1875 Daniel Seiler, he was born May 2, 1853
       and he died Aug. 22, 1913 (MC).

CLARISSA JANE-9 CROASMUN, b. Jan. 5, 1854 (MC);
    d. Sept. 5, 1855 (MC); died 1 year 8 months (MC).

see page
522 JAMES ASBURY-9 CROASMUN, b. May 3, 1853 (MC);
    d.
    m. Agnes Oberlin, she was born May 3, 1858 (MC).

see page
523 MARY ELIZABETH-9 CROASMUN, b. Nov. 13, 1856 (MC);
    d. Aug. 2, 1938 (MC);
    m. Aug. 31, 1880 John Paul Enterline, he was born Sept.
       11, 1853 and died Jan. 10, 1942 (MC).

see page
524 ANNA CAROLINE-9 CROASMUN, b. March 25, 1860 (MC);
    d.
    m. Hulette A. Smith (MC).

see page
525 EVERETT LINCOLN-9 CROASMUN, b. March 21, 1862 (MC);
    d. May 24, 1944 (MC);
    m. July 7, 1887 Mary Alice Fetteroff, she was born Oct.
       2, 1864 and died Aug. 16, 1930 (MC).

see page
526 ISAAC McHENRY-9 CROASMUN, b. Aug. 13, 1869 (MC);
    d. Feb. 6, 1956 (MC);
    m. Oct. 1, 1891 Mary L. Zufall, she was born Aug. 24,
       1870 and died in 1905 (MC).

see page
527 AUGUSTA HELEN-9 CROASMUN, b.Jan. 19, 1864 (MC);
    d.
    m. Charley A. Oberlin, he was born Jan. 11, 1857 and
       died May 8, 1940 (MC).

see page
528 SUSAN JOSEPHINE-9 CROASMUN, b. Jan. 18, 1866 (MC);
    d. Oct.   1947 (MC);
    m. May 14, 1889 Marim Seldon Stevens, he was born Aug.
       30, 1854 and he died May 13, 1936 (MC).

****

see page
491

MILES-8 CROASMUN (Asa-7, Asa-6, James-5, Joseph-4, Joseph-3,
                                   Robert-2, John-1)

b. Sept. 10, 1831 (MC);
d. Sept. 12, 1917, buried at White Churchyard, Hamilton, PA (MC);
m. Jan. 5, 1871 Margaret Jane Beck, she was born July 23,
   1844 and died March 31, 1939 (MC).

CHILDREN:

GEORGE ALLEN-9 CROASMUN, b. Oct. 7, 1871 (MC);
   d. Jan. 12, 1872, died in infancy (MC).

see page
529
MARY OLIVE-9 CROASMUN, b. May 24, 1873 twin (MC);
   d. March 17, 1962 (MC);
   m. June 18, 1902 Isaac Curtis Dormire, he was born April
      28, 1876 and died Nov. 4, 1956 (MC).

MARGARET ELVIRA-9 CROASMUN, b. May 24, 1873, twin (MC);
   d. Nov. 30, 1938 (MC);
   m. unmarried (MC).

see page
530
WILLIAM CLARK-9 CROASMUN, b. Feb. 3, 1876 (MC);
   d. Jan. 16, 1959 (MC);
   m. June 22, 1904 Clara Grace Gilmore, "Polly" was born
      May 24, 1889 (MC); divorced (MC);
   m.(2) Dec. 22, 1920 Sara Elizabeth "Sophie" Martin, she
      was born Feb. 18, 1884 and died Sept. 13, 1971 (MC).

see page
531
NATHAN BURTON-9 CROASMUN, b. Jan. 3, 1879 (MC); twin (MC);
   d. Dec. 20, 1964 (MC);
   m. Dec. 17, 1908 Belva Jane Blakely, she was born Oct.
      23, 1884 and died June 2, 1973 (MC).

ASA MURTON-9 CROASMUN, b. Jan. 3, 1879, twin (MC);
   d. Dec. 24, 1962 (MC);
   m. Feb. 24, 1916 Lucinda Gertrude Henry, she was born
      April 28, 1882 and died Jan. 2, 1938 (MC).
   m.(2) Aug. 15, 1941 Blanche Cook-Hetriek-Wannerd, she
      was born April 14, 1878 and died April 1, 1964 (MC).

   CHILDREN: (OF ASA AND LUCINDA)

KATHLEEN JANE-10 CROASMUN, b. Oct. 31, 1919 (MC);
   m. Wendell Thomas Haughton, retired Captain (MC);
      they live at 1207 Mississippi Ave., Silver City,
      New Mexico 88061 (MC).

   CHILDREN: (OF KATHLEEN AND WENDELL)

THOMAS WENDELL-11 HAUGHTON, b. Nov. 1, 1950 (MC).

****

JAMES WASHINGTON-8 CROASMUN   (Asa-7, Asa-6,   James-5, Joseph-4, Joseph-3,
Robert-2, John-1)

b. Nov. 9, 1834 (MC);
d. March 26, 1911 (MC);
m.   1857 Julia Ann Sutter, she was born Aug. 5,
    1842 and died July 26, 1916 (MC).

CHILDREN:

ARABELLA JANE "Jennie"-9 CROASMUN, b. Dec. 21, 1861 (MC);
    d. Nov. 23, 1948 (MC);
    m. Aug. 3, 1881 Allen Wallace, he was born Nov., 1856
        and he died Sept. 16, 1916 (MC).

    CHILDREN:

    JOANNA FAYE-10 WALLACE, b. Jan. 11, 1883 (MC);
        d. Jan. 21, 1930 (MC);
        m. May 12, 1901 Joseph Clyde Gilbert, he was born
            1878 and died Nov. 27, 1933 (MC).

        CHILDREN:

        ADDA WILHELMINA-11 GILBERT, b. Nov. 15, 1902 (MC);
            m. 1934 Samuel Stevenson (MC).

see page
532 DANIEL HENRY-9 CROASMUN, b. June 28, 1866, twin (MC);
        d. July 5, 1946 (MC);
    m. Oct. 8, 1886 Effie Margaret Mauk, she was born Nov.
        28, 1868 and died Nov. 15, 1944 (MC).

REBECCA ADDA-9 CROASMUN, b. June 28, 1866, twin (MC);
    d. Sept.   1947 (MC);
    m. May 1, 1894 Charles Lafayette Moss, he was born
        in 1862 (MC).

****

see page
491

ELIZABETH JANE-8 CROASMUN   (Asa-7, Asa-6, James-5, Joseph-4, Joseph-3, Robert-2, John-1)

b. April 24 or 25, 1842 (MC);
d. April 23, 1902 (MC);
m.   James Madison Chambers, he was born
   Dec. 23 or 27, 1844 and he died June 6 or Jan. 6,1915(MC).

CHILDREN:

see page
533
HARRY NEWTON-9 CHAMBERS, b. Dec. 5, 1867 (MC);
      d. 1941 (MC);
      m. Nov. 28, 1895 Mary Olive Sprankle, she was born
         Feb. 7, 1873 and died Jan. 1963 (MC).

see page
534
ANNA DORA-9 CHAMBERS, b.April 5, 1868 (MC);
      d. Sept. 1939 (MC); never married (MC).

MARY INEZ-9 CHAMBERS, b. April 18, 1871 (MC);
   d. April 22, 1892 (MC).

LILY JANE-9 CHAMBERS, b. Feb. 2, 1873 (MC);
   d. Sept. 18, 1877, died in childhood (MC).

see page
535
ZIELA BLANCHE-9 CHAMBERS, Sept. 17, 1875, twin (MC);
      d. Sept.   1957 (MC);
      m. Sept. 17, 1903 Harvey Jacob Dormire, he was born
         Jan. 29, 1879 and he disappeared with no record
         in 1931 or 1932 (MC).

see page
536
MILES BLANCHARD-9 CHAMBERS, b. Sept. 17, 1875 (MC);
      d. April   1954 (MC);
      m.   Carrie Dorothea Jordon, she was
         born in May 21, 1878 and died May 15, 1972 (MC).

see page
537
ETHEL MARGRETTA-9 CHAMBERS, b. March 29, 1879 (MC);
      d. June 20, 1956 (MC);
      m. May 1, 1900 William Sheridan Shaffer, he was born
         Sept. 5, 1871 and died May 17, 1956 (MC).

see page
538
JAMES ASA GARFIELD-9 CHAMBERS, b.Jan. 31,1881 (MC);
      d. April 24, 1932 (MC);
      m. Dec. 18, 1909 Mabel Etta McConaughy, she was born
         July 30, 1889 and died Dec. 8, 1947 (MC).

see page
539
AUGUSTA MAUD-9 CHAMBERS, b. Nov. 10, 1885 (MC);
      d. still living in 1978 (MC);
      m. May 11, 1910 Edward Lee Fleming, he was a Doctor,
         born Sept. 21, 1884 and died ? (MC).

****

**This page is intentionally blank
to allow the next generation
to begin on a right hand page.**

Our
Ninth
Generation

Page Number

ESTHER OLIVE-9 PIPER   (William-8, Rebecca-7, Asa-6,
                        James-5, Joseph-4, Joseph-3,
                        Robert-2, John-1)

b.   1864 (AD);
d.   1942 (AD);
m.   1884 Monroe Denman, he was born 1856 and died
     in 1932. They had five children (AD).

     Esther Olive Piper came to Spokane County in 1884 and
Monroe Denman came to Spokane Co., in 1879 before the
railroad came thru.

     CHILDREN:

CLARENCE LUCIUS-10 DENMAN,b. 1885 in Spokane Co.(AD);
     d. 1898 "same from hurt" (AD).

DORANCE ORVICE-10 DENMAN,b. 1888 in Spokane Co. (AD);
     d.
     m. 1910 Lela Brown in Hillyard, Washington.(AD);
        They had three daughters (AD).

see page
540 ALFRED MONROE-10 DENMAN, b. 1892 in Hillyard, Wash.(AD);
     d. still living in 1977 in Spokane, Washington;
     m. 1914 Lillie Rose (AD).

ENOS C.-10 DENMAN, b.
     d.
     m. three times (AD); had no children (AD).

GROVE BLAINE-10 DENMAN, b. 1907 (AD);
     d.
     m. twice and had a daughter (AD).

OREGON ELLSWORTH-9 CROASMAN   (James-8, Joseph-7, Asa-6,
                                James-5, Joseph-4, Joseph-3,
                                Robert-2, John-1)
b.   Jan. 11, 1865 in Oregon (BS);
d.   *June 13, 1935 (BS)*

m.   Jan. 18,1900 Helen Gay King (MC).

   CHILDREN:

DORIS MAXINE-10 CROASMAN, b.May 27, 1905 (MC);
   d.
   m. Irving Lester Baumann (MC).

      CHILDREN:

         BARBARA-11 BAUMANN, b.Feb.3,1930(MC);
           m.June 1, 1952 Joaquin William "J.W." Silveira(MC).

            CHILDREN:

               WILLIAM-12 SILVEIRA, b.March 12,1957 (MC).

               BRIAN-12 SILVEIRA, b.Aug.25,1959 (MC).

Genealogy of the Crossman Family, Supplement #3 · ©1990 by Robert Owen Crossman · 908 Front · Conway, AR 72032

MARY ELIZA-9 CRISSMAN   (Mary-8, Asa-7, Asa-6,
                        James-5, Joseph-4, Joseph-3,
                        Robert-2, John-1)

b.
d.
m.   Michael Lantz (MC). They had one child.

    CHILDREN:

MARGARET "Maggie"-10 LANTZ, b.
    d.
    m.   Washington J. Hicks (MC).
      They had seven children.

    CHILDREN:

see page
582 LAWRENCE-11 HICKS, b.
         d.
         m. Vesta Craig (MC). Lived in Indiana Co.,PA.(MC).

see page
583 LEONARD GUY-11 HICKS, b.
         d.
         m. Ida Summers (MC).

see page
584 LILLIAN-11 HICKS, b.
         d.
         m. Emaus Gould (MC). Lived in Redwood City, Calf.(MC).

see page
585 BESSIE V.-11 HICKS, b.April 12, 1888 (MC);
         d. June 10, 1970 (MC);
         m. William J. Kerr (MC).

       BLAIR-11 HICKS, b.
         d.
         m. unmarried (MC).

see page
586 ALMA-11 HICKS, b.
         d.
         m. Raymond Martin (MC).

see page
587 VADA-11 HICKS, b.
         d.
         m. Joseph Fetterhoff (MC).
            Lived in Plumville, Pennsylvania (MC).

ELIZABETH ANN-9 BARRACK   (Mary-8, Asa-7, Asa-6,
                          James-5, Joseph-4, Joseph-3,
                          Robert-2, John-1)

    b. May 26, 1853 (MC);
    d. Feb. 6, 1924 (MC);
    m. Dec. 28, 1877 or 1876 Abram Hicks, he was born on
       July 15, 1852 and died Nov. 29, 1920 (MC).

    CHILDREN:

see page
541 JESSIE WILLIAM "J.W."-10 HICKS, b.Oct.22,1878 (MC);
        d.
        m.(1) Lana Postewaite, she was born Oct.27,1876 and
              she died in 1902 (MC);
        m.(2) Sarah Elizabeth Neil (MC).

see page
542 MARY ADDA VERNA-10 HICKS, b. Nov. 23, 1880 (MC);
        d.
        m. Dec.   1906 David Anthony Gross, he died June
           13, 1929 (MC).

     AVIS EARL-10 HICKS, b.Dec. 8, 1882 (MC);
        d.
        m. Carrie Wall (MC). No children (MC).

see page
543 PRESTON BARRACK-10 HICKS, b. Oct. 30, 1884 (MC);
        d.
        m. Dollie L. Lamison (MC).

see page
544 LUCRIETIA MAUD-10 HICKS, b. Nov. 23, 1886 (MC);
        d.
        m. Feb. 4, 1907 John Gourley Crawford, he was born
           March 8, 1884 (MC).

     MABEL INEZ-10 HICKS, b.Feb. 19, 1889 (MC);
        d.
        m. unmarried (MC).

     INFANT-10 HICKS, b. Aug. 19, 1891 (MC);
        d. Aug. 19, 1891 at birth (MC).

     MILES-10 HICKS, b. May 15, 1893 (MC);
        d.Aug.   1893 (MC); died in infancy (MC).

see page
546 ERNIE MARGARET-10 HICKS, b.July 7, 1894 (MC);
        d.
        m. John Myers (MC).

     BOYD-10 HICKS, b.   (MC)
        d.
        m.

see page
502

MATILDA JANE "Jennie"-9 ROBINSON   (Mary-8, Asa-7, Asa-6,
                                    James-5, Joseph-4, Joseph-3,
                                    Robert-2, John-1)

b. Jan. 17, 1857 (MC);
d. Aug. 19, 1929 (MC);
m. March 12, 1874 Michael Harwick (or Harwig), he was born
   Dec. 29, 1854 and died Oct.   1940 (MC).

CHILDREN:

WILLIAM BRYAN-10 HARWICK, b.May 25, 1875 (MC);
     d. Nov. 28, 1956 (MC);
     m. Nov. 21, 1906 Sara "Ada" Postwaite, she was born
        July 10, 1882 (MC).
        CHILDREN:
           SARAH "Edith" AZALEA-11 HARWICK, b.April 3,1910(MC);
              unmarried and lived in Valier, PA (MC).

see page
547
MARY M.-10 HARWICK, b.Oct. 7, 1877 (MC);
     d.Feb. 12, 1904 (MC);
     m.July 8, 1897 W. Edward Heitzenrater

see page
548
MELISSA GERTRUDE-10 HARWICK, b.July 8, 1879 (MC);
     d. Feb. 26, 1904 (MC);
     m. Jan. 17, 1902 M_____ Depp (MC).

see page
549
JAMES J.-10 HARWICK, b.Sept. 19, 1881 (MC);
     d.
     m. April 27, 1907 Eva "Mae Nie" Lydic (MC).

INFANT SON-10 HARWICK, b. Feb. 18, 1885 (MC);
     d. Feb. 19, 1885 (MC), died in infancy (MC).

see page
550
ALBERT BARTON-10 HARWICK, b.July 19, 1886 (MC);
     d. July 22, 1964 (MC);
     m. July 4, 1906 Myrtle Bush, she was born March 15,1889,
        interviewed by Marion Croasmun on Sept. 7, 1977 (MC).

ALMA ELIZABETH-10 HARWICK, b.July 24, 1889 (MC);
     d.
     m.March 4, 1910 David Steel (MC).
        CHILDREN:
           INFANT DAUGHTER-11 STEEL, b.July 12, 1910 (MC);
              d.July 12, 1910, died day of birth (MC).
           HAROLD HARWICK-11 STEEL, b.March 9, 1914 (MC).

ANDREW P.-10 HARWICK, b.Sept,29,1895 (MC);
     d.
     m.Sept. 3,1919 Millie Neal (MC).
        CHILDREN:
           RICHARD-11 HARWICK, b.   (MC)
             m. Dolores Baker (MC).
           CHARLES BARTON "Barry"-11 HARWICK, b.   (MC).

JENNIE B.-10 HARWICK, b. Oct. 4, 1900 (MC);
     d. Dec. 21, 1903 in childhood (MC).

****
514

EVALINE-9 CROSSMAN (Isaac-8, Asa-7, Asa-6, James-5, Joseph-4, Joseph-3,
                                        Robert-2, John-1)

   b. Sept. 8, 1847 (MC);
   d. Aug. 11, 1874 (MC);
   m. Nov.   1867 William E. Vandermark (MC).

      CHILDREN:

JOHN-10 VANDERMARK, b.July 28, 1871 (MC);
   d. Aug. 2, 1903 (MC);
   m. unmarried (MC).

GEORGE SHARP-10 VANDERMARK, b.Nov. 28, 1872 (MC);
   d.
   m. Jan. 12, 1898 Jennie Smith, she was born May 5, 1876
      and she died Aug. 29, 1922 (MC).

   CHILDREN:

      EDGAR-11 VANDERMARK, b. May 18, 1900 (MC);
         d.
      m. Oct. 16, 1922 Mary Neff, she was born Oct.8,
         1903 (MC).

         CHILDREN:

            LEE SMITH-12 VANDERMARK, b. Feb. 24, 1931 (MC);
               d.

            JOHN-12 VANDERMARK, b.   (MC).

      HELEN-11 VANDERMARK, b. July 14, 1902 (MC);
         d. July 13, 1903, died at one year (MC).

              ****

GEORGE GRANT-9 CROSSMAN (Isaac-8, Asa-7, Asa-6,
                         James-5, Joseph-4, Joseph-3,
                         Robert-2, John-1)
b. Feb. 9 or 24, 1862 (MC);
d. Jan. 24, 1941 (MC);
m. April 7, 1892 Mary Ellen "Nellie" M Dodge, she was
   born March 25, 1871 and died March 23, 1951 (MC).

   CHILDREN:

RUTH-10 CROSSMAN, b. Nov. 26, 1893 (MC);
   d. Nov. 26, 1893 died at birth (MC).

see page
551 WILLIAM CLARK-10 CROSSMAN, b. Dec. 14, 1894 (MC);
   d.
   m. Feb. 20, 1926 Mary Holliman, she was born April 11,
      1905 (MC).
   They live at Vienna, Virginia (MC).

see page
552 FLORENCE CELESTE-10 CROSSMAN, b. Nov. 24,1897 (MC);
   d.
   m. Nov. 30, 1923 Frank Romine Taylor, he was born
      Oct. 1, 1897 (MC).

see page
553 GEORGE ISAAC-10 CROSSMAN, b. Dec. 5, 1900 (MC);
   d.
   m. May 15, 1925 Bessie M. Diefenbach, she was born
      Aug. 20, 1903 (MC).

MARY LOUISE-10 CROSSMAN, b. July 1, 1903 (MC);
   d.
   m.(1) Dec. 30, 1928 Stanley Francis White (divorced)(MC);
   m.(2) Oct. 1, 1933 Otis E. Shaw, he was born Nov. 9,
      1903 (MC).

JULIAN-10 CROSSMAN, b. May 25, 1908 (MC);
   d. June 1, 1908, died in infancy (MC).

****

Genealogy of the Crossman Family, Supplement #3 • ©1990 by Robert Owen Crossman • 908 Front • Conway, AR 72032

see page
505

INA MAUD-9 CROASMUN   (Nathan-8, Asa-7, Asa-6,
                      James-5, Joseph-4, Joseph-3,
                      Robert-2, John-1)
b. Oct. 12, 1863 (MC);
d. Oct. 24, 1934, buried at Barretts Chapel, Delaware (MC);
m. Sept. 2, 1891 Howard Bruce Defibaugh, he was born Sept.
   17, 1864 and died Nov. 17, 1927 (MC).

CHILDREN:

NATHAN CLYDE-10 DEFIBAUGH, b. Dec. 12, 1892 Clayville,PA(MC);
   d. Aug. 26, 1977 (MC);
   m. Nov. 1, 1923 Elsie Amelia Potts, she was born Oct.
      25, 1907 (MC); No children (MC); retirement address
      62 Sunny Shore Drive, Ormond Beach, Florida 32074.

HOWARD CLAIR-10 DEFIBAUGH, b. April 10, 1898 (MC);
   d. April,   1957 (MC); lived at Woodside Delaware(MC);
   m.   Elizabeth Stewart (MC).
   Children:
      IRENE IOLA-11 DEFIBAUGH, b.Aug.17,1921(MC);
         m.Feb.1,1941 Olive Merwin Kersey, born April 18,1918.
         Children:
            HARVEY CLAIR-12 KERSEY, b.Nov.4,1942 (MC).
               Children:
                  TONI ELIZABETH-13 KERSEY, b.Feb.10,1963 (MC).
                  JULIA MICHELLE-13 KERSEY, b.March 14,1965 (MC).
            SANDRA JEAN-12 KERSEY, b.Feb.20,1947; m.__Hughes.
               Children:
                  KELLY RENEE-13 HUGHES, b.July 5, 1965 (MC).
                  HEATHER MARLYN-13 HUGHES, b.Aug.15,1967(MC).
      ELIZABETH "Betty"CLAIR-11 DEFIBAUGH, b.Jan.21,1923(MC);
         m.Dec.31,1942 Titus M. Bush, born March 24,1914 (MC).
         Children:
            HOWARD MEREDITH-12 BUSH, b.Oct.3,1943 (MC).
            MICHAEL FITZGERALD-12 BUSH, b.Oct.2,1947 (MC).
      FRANCES GERALDINE-11 DEFIBAUGH, b.Jan.24,1924 (MC);
         m.March 18,1945 John Hazal Johnson Cook, he was
            born Feb. 16, 1920 (MC).
         Children:
            PAMELA STEWART-12 COOK, b. Oct. 23, 1950 (MC).
      JEAN LOUISE-11 DEFIBAUGH, b.Dec.22,1930 (MC);
         m.Oct.28,1950 Milton Stakely Griffith Jr., born
            Sept. 3, ____ (MC).
         Children:
            STACEY LYNN-12 GRIFFITH, b. Aug. 13, 1951 (MC).
            ANDREA JEAN-12 GRIFFITH, b. Jan. 10, 1952 (MC).
            MELTON STAKELY-12 GRIFFITH III, b.Aug.27,1957 (MC).
            SHAWN LORRAINE-12 GRIFFITH, b. Oct. 9, 1959 (MC).
            ROBERT SPENCE-12 GRIFFITH, b. Jan. 4, 1965 (MC).

see page
505

DARIUS MILES "Desi"-9 CROASMUN   (Nathan-8, Asa-7, Asa-6,
                                 James-5, Joseph-4, Joseph-3,
                                 Robert-2, John-1)

b. June 20, 1866 (MC);
d. Jan. 3, 1943 (MC);
m. Dec. 26, 1889 Miranda McHenry, she was born Dec. 6,
   1867 and died Sept. 23, 1897 (MC).

CHILDREN:

MARY NEVADA-10 CROASMUN, b.Nov. or Dec. 25,1890 (MC);
   d. Aug. 11, 1926 (MC);
   m. Nov. 28, 1922 Henry Halberg, he was born April 9,
      1891 and died Aug. 5, 1970 (MC); Henry remarried
      to a Lovine Anderson after Mary's death (MC).
Children:

   GERALDINE "Jane"-11 HALBERG, b.Nov.13,1923 (MC);
      m.____ Buffa (MC).

   FRANCES GERTRUDE-11 HALBERG, b.Dec.31,1925 (MC);
      m. Elmer Gamble (MC).
      Children:

         LINDA LOU-12 GAMBLE, b. Feb. 9, 1955 (MC).

         SANDRA SUE-12 GAMBLE, b. June 17, 1959 (MC).

HARRY-10 CROASMUN, b. Aug. 29, 1892 (MC);
   d. Jan. 19, 1893, died in infancy (MC).

****

see page
506

HENRIETTA MARIA-9 CROASMUN   (Asa-8, Asa-7, Asa-6,
                              James-5, Joseph-4, Joseph-3,
                              Robert-2, John-1)
   b. July 4, 1852 (MC);
   d. March 12, 1932 (MC);
   m. Nov. 27, 1875 Daniel Seiler, he was born May 2, 1853
      and he died Aug. 22, 1913 (MC).

      CHILDREN:

ISAAC PRESTON-10 SEILER, b. Nov. 27, 1875 (MC);
   d. Jan. 25, 1944 (MC);
   m. Oct.   , 1903 Ethel Louise Dewey, she died June 26,1927.
   m.(2) Nov. 25, 1929 Rose Olekush (MC).
   Children:
      JACK DEWEY-11 SEILER, b.   ; m. Beatrice_____(MC).
         Children:
            WILLIAM PRESTON-12 SEILER, b. May 3,1944 (MC).
            ETHEL LOUISE "Judy"-12 SEILER, b.Nov.12,1945 (MC).

see page
558

IRA DWIGHT-10 SEILER, b. Oct. 16, 1877 (MC);
   d. Aug. 9, 1957 (MC);
   m. Dec.,   1903 Jessie Shepherd (MC);
   m.(1) Christine Swanson (MC);
   m.(3) Alda Warren (MC).

IDA MARY "Belle"-10 SEILER, b. Oct. 16, 1877 (MC);
   d. Aug. 7, 1947 (MC);
   m. May 5, 1913 Ernest W. Moyer, he was born July 5, 1875
      and he died Fall of 1962 (MC).
   Children:
      LUCILLE-11 MOYER, b. Feb. 14, 1914, twin (MC);
         m.Sept. 15,1940 Robert C. Owens, he was born Oct.
         25, 1911 and died Feb. 7,1949 (MC). They lived in
         Portland, Oregon (MC).
      LOUISE-11 MOYER, b. Feb.14,1914, twin (MC);
         m. May 23, 1943 John W. Wood, he was born Sept. 8,
            1912 (MC); they live in Heppner, Oregon (MC).
         Children:
            JAMES WALTER-12 WOOD, b.March 12, 1947 (MC);
               m.Aug. 1969 Jean Stockard (MC).
      CAROLINE-11 MOYER, b.March 23, 1915 (MC); unmarried(MC);
         she received a A.B. from Greely College and an
         M.A. from the University of Oregon (MC).
      MIRIAM-11 MOYER, b. May 15, 1916 (MC);
         m.April 5, 1947 Jack W. Carmichael, he was born
            April 10,1922 and lives in Santa Barbara, Calf.(MC).
      JOHN DANIEL-11 MOYER, b.March 21, 1917, twin (MC);
         d. July 7, 1917, died in infancy (MC).
      PHILIP DAVID-11 MOYER, b. March 21, 1917, twin (MC);
         d. March 29, 1917, died in infancy (MC).
      JAMES H.-11 MOYER, b. March 20, 1920 (MC);
         d. March   , 19__ (MC).
IVAN CARL-10 SEILER, b. Dec.25,1881 (MC); d.Feb.11,1941(MC);
   m.June 5,1901 Nora Ida Eisenhart, b. Jan.2,1901 (MC).
   Children:
      MARY-11 SEILER, b. m.Carl Stewart (MC).
         Children:
            YVONNE-12 STEWART, b. 1934 (MC).
      RICHARD-11 SEILER, b.   (MC).
MARION SELDOM STEVEN-10 SEILER, b.March 11, 1889 (MC);
   m.March 18,1925 Marie See (MC).
          ****

JAMES ASBURY-9 CROASMUN   (Asa-8, Asa-7, Asa-6,
                          James-5, Joseph-4, Joseph-3,
                          Robert-2, John-1)
b. May 3, 1853 (MC);
d.
m. Agnes Oberlin, she was born May 3, 1858 (MC).

   CHILDREN:

LESBIA C.-10 CROASMUN, b.
    m. Earl Rigg (MC).
    Children:
      JAMES-11 RIGG, b.
        m. Ruth Stephens (MC).
        Children:
          JACQUELIN CLAIR-12 RIGG, b.   (MC).
          DONALD CLYDE-12 RIGG, b.   (MC).

CHARLOTTE-10 CROASMUN, b.
    d. July 31, 1971 (MC);
    m. Clyde Seanar (MC).

GERTRUDE-10 CROASMUN, b.
    d.
    m. John Hickman (MC).
    Children:
      AGNES MARY-11 HICKMAN, b.
        d.
        m. Elbert Hargeshimer (MC).
        Children:
          ELBERT-12 HARGESHIMER, b.   (MC).

          BECKY-12 HARGESHIMER, b.   (MC).

          JOHN MICHAEL-12 HARGESHIMER, b.   (MC).

MARY ELIZABETH-9 CROASMUN   (Asa-8, Asa-7, Asa-6,
                             James-5, Joseph-4, Joseph-3,
                             Robert-2, John-1)
b. Nov. 13, 1856 (MC);
d. Aug. 2, 1938 (MC);
m. Aug. 31, 1880 John Paul Enterline, he was born Sept.
   11, 1853 and died Jan. 10, 1942 (MC).

     CHILDREN:

see page
559 THOMAS O.-10 ENTERLINE, b. March 7, 1883 (MC);
          d. April 8, 1966 (MC);
          m. June 28, 1911 Zelda Rae Kuntz, she was born Jan.
             30, 1889 (MC).

MERVYN ORVAL-10 ENTERLINE, b. June 18, 1885 (MC);
     d. Feb. 22, 1968 (MC);
     m. Virginia Mieler (MC).
     Children:

        JOHN "Jack"-11 ENTERLINE, b.
          m. Rose Mary Bennett (MC).
          Children:
             JUDITH ANN-12 ENTERLINE, b. July 18, 1944 (MC).

             JACK LAWRENCE-12 ENTERLINE, b. Oct. 18, 1945 (MC).

             JON LESLIE-12 ENTERLINE, b. Oct. 17, 1947 (MC).

             JIL-12 ENTERLINE, b.   (MC).

        JOSEPH CROASMUN-11 ENTERLINE, b. March 14, 1921 (MC);
          d.
          m. Helen May Finney (MC).
          Children:

             DIANA KERNEY-12 ENTERLINE, b. April 19, 1953 (MC).

                    ****

see page
506

ANNA CAROLINE-9 CROASMUN   (Asa-8, Asa-7, Asa-6,
                            James-5, Joseph-4, Joseph-3,
                            Robert-2, John-1)

b. March 25, 1860 (MC);
d.
m.   Hulette A. Smith (MC).

   CHILDREN:

JASPER-10 SMITH, b.   (MC);
   d.
   m.

BERTHA-10 SMITH, b.   (MC).

BURTON-10 SMITH, b.   (MC).

ETTA-10 SMITH, b.   (MC).

EARL-10 SMITH, b.   (MC).

BLAKE-10 SMITH, b.   (MC).

****

see page
506

EVERETT LINCOLN-9 CROASMUN   (Asa-8, Asa-7, Asa-6,
                             James-5, Joseph-4, Joseph-3,
                             Robert-2, John-1)

b. March 21, 1862 (MC);
d. May 24, 1944 (MC);
m. July 7, 1887 Mary Alice Fetteroff, she was born Oct.
   2, 1864 and died Aug. 16, 1930 (MC).

   CHILDREN:

see page
560
EFFA BEULAH-10 CROASMUN, b. Feb. 17, 1888 (MC);
     d. July 7, 1963 (MC);
   m. Dec. 25,1915 Harry Leroy Ramaley (MC).

see page
561
PAUL STEVENS-10 CROASMUN, b. Dec. 18, 1890 (MC);
     d.
   m. June 15, 1918 Margaret Seitz, she was born Dec.
      3, 1889 (MC).

see page
562
NANNIE LULA-10 CROASMUN, b. Jan. 2, 1893 (MC);
     d. Aug. 19, 1963 (MC);
   m. April 12, 1916 J. Boyd Smith, he was born Sept.
      28, 1894 and died Jan. 13, 1978 (MC).

see page
563
TWILA BELLE-10 CROASMUN, b. April 26, 1895 (MC);
     d. Aug. 10, 1977 (MC);
   m. James Carl Neal, he was born May 31, 1897, they
      were married on Sept. 28, 1918 (MC).

****

525

see page
506

ISAAC McHENRY-9 CROASMUN   (Asa-8, Asa-7, Asa-6,
                          James-5, Joseph-4, Joseph-3,
                          Robert-2, John-1)
b. Aug. 13, 1869 (MC);
d. Feb. 6, 1956 (MC);
m. Oct. 1, 1891 Mary L. Zufall, she was born Aug. 24, 1870
   and she died in 1905 (MC).

   CHILDREN:

ELSIE-10 CROASMUN, b.
   m. Reed Lettie (MC).
   Children:
      CHILD-11 LETTIE, b.   ; d.with mother at birth (MC).

see page
564
NAOMI-10 CROASMUN, b. April 27, 1894 (MC);
        d.
   m. Nov. 24, 1915 John C. Emhoff, b.Dec.11,1896 (MC).

CHARLES G.-10 CROASMUN, b. Oct.7,1895 (MC);
   d. July 4, 1974 (MC);
   m. Kathryn M. Zoller, b. Jan. 18, 1897 (MC).
   Children:
      CHARLES G.-11 CROASMUN, Jr., b.Dec.22, 1924 (MC);
        m. Lios Allene Evans (MC).
        Children:
           KAREN L.-12 CROASMUN, b.Feb. 12, 1952 (MC).
           LESLIE A.-12 CROASMUN, b. April 17, 1954 (MC).
           DEBRA L.-12 CROASMUN, b. Sept. 19, 1956 (MC).
           SCOTT B.-12 CROASMUN, b. April 12, 1959 (MC).
      JEAN L.-11 CROASMUN, b. Aug. 19, 1936 (MC);
        m. Gerald Davis (MC); live in New Mexico (MC).
        Children:
           DEBBIE JEAN-12 DAVIS, b. April 10, 1958 (MC).
           EDWARD C.-12 DAVIS, b. Dec. 21, 1961 (MC).
           SHARON P.-12 DAVIS, b. March 18, 1962 (MC).

SARABELLE-10 CROASMUN, b. March 7, 1899 (MC);
   d.
   m. Charles Stitler (MC).
   Children:
      CHARLES-11 STITLER, b. March 6, 1918 (MC);
         m. Bettie_____(MC).
      TERRY-11 STITLER, b.   (MC).
      JACK-11 STITLER, b.   (MC).

****

see page
506

AUGUSTA HELEN-9 CROASMUN (Asa-8, Asa-7, Asa-6,
                          James-5, Joseph-4, Joseph-3,
                          Robert-2, John-1)
    b. Jan. 19, 1864 (MC);
    d.
    m.   Charley A. Oberlin, he was born on
        Jan. 11, 1857 and he died May 8, 1940 (MC).

        CHILDREN:

see page
565
MABEL FLORENCE-10 OBERLIN, b. Nov.30,1884 (MC);
        d. May 4, 1970 (MC);
        m.   1901 Lester E. Faulk, he died in 1966 (MC).

    CLYDE ALBERT-10 OBERLIN, b. 1887 (MC);
        d. 1909 (MC); unmarried (MC).

    SEILER DANIEL-10 OBERLIN, b.1888 (MC);
        d. 1962 (MC);
        m. Emma F. Freas
            Children:

                daughter-11 OBERLIN, b.   (MC);
                  m. Turner Carpenter (MC).
                  they have two children (MC).

    IRENE-10 OBERLIN, b.   1889 (MC);
        d. 1918 (MC);
        m. A.B. Holyfield (MC).

        Children:

            CHARLES-11 HOLYFIELD, b.   (MC).
                d.
                m.
                  Children:

                    they have two daughters and one son (MC).

            ****

527

SUSAN JOSEPHINE-9 CROASMUN   (Asa-8, Asa-7, Asa-6,
                                James-5, Joseph-4, Joseph-3,
                                Robert-2, John-1)

b. Jan. 18, 1866 (MC);
d. Oct.   1947 (MC);
m. May 14, 1889 Marim Seldon Stevens, he was born Aug.
   30, 1854 and died May 13, 1936 (MC).

   CHILDREN:

MARION-10 STEVENS , b. Aug. 9, 1890 (MC);
   d.
   m. March 14, 1912 Paul M. Reidy, he was born 1871 and
      he died in 1940 (MC).
   Marion lives in Los Angeles, California (MC).
   Children:
     ELLA MAE-11 REIDY, b. Dec. 28,1911 (MC);
       m. Thomas Manwarring, he was born Dec. 9, 1904 and
          he died April   1963 (MC); no children (MC);
          Ella Mae lives in Los Angeles, California (MC).
     MARIAN PAULINE-11 REIDY, b. Dec. 31, 1918 (MC).
       m. Dr. Stewart King (MC).
       Children:
         MICHAEL-12 KING, b. 1943 (MC).

         KORTLAND-12 KING, b. April 21, 1949 (MC).
LLOYD C.-10 STEVENS, b. April 30, 1894 (MC);
   d.
   m. Dec. 20, 1920 Reba Bland, she was born Feb. 4,1892(MC);
      They live in Piedmont, California (MC).
   Children:
     SALLY-11 STEVENS, b.   (MC);
       m.   Waldo (MC).

     FRANCES-11 STEVENS, b.   (MC);
       m.   (MC).
       Children:

         WENDY-12 WALDO, b. 1949 (MC).

see page 566 SUE MAURINE-10 STEVENS, b. 1901 (MC);
       m. 1928 Richard Howard Morrison, b. 1896 and d.1939(MC).

PATRICIA LUCILLE "Queenie"-10 STEVENS, b. Aug. 12,1905(MC);
   d. Sept. 15, 1968 (MC);
   m. Aug. 12, 1957 Howard Erving, he was born 1881 and he
      died June 18, 1967 (MC); no children (MC).

****

MARY OLIVE-9 CROASMUN,   (Miles-8, Asa-7, Asa-6,
James-5, Joseph-4, Joseph-3,
Robert-2, John-1)
b. May 24, 1873, twin (MC);
d. March 17, 1962 (MC);
m. June 18, 1902 Isaac Curtis Dormire, he was born April
   28, 1876 and died Nov. 4, 1956 (MC).

CHILDREN:

see page
567
ELIZABETH BLANCHE-10 DORMIRE, b. June 21, 1903 (MC);
   d.
   m. April 29, 1939 John Quincey Hoover, he was born
      Dec. 23, 1901 (MC).

MARGARET RUTH "Peg"-10 DORMIRE, b. Sept. 8, 1905 (MC);
   d.
   m. Sept. 1, 1930 Wilfred Edmondson, he was born Jan.
      29, 1902 (MC).
   Children:
     WILFRED ALLEN-11 EDMUNDSON, b. Dec. 4, 1934 (MC);
        d. April 12, 1945 in childhood (MC).

     SHIRLEY LEE-11 EDMUNDSON, b. May 19, 1937 (MC);
        Shirley works as a registered nurse (MC).

see page
568
MARY ELVIRA-10 DORMIRE, b. Aug. 30, 1909 (MC);
   d.
   m. June 1, 1933 Robert Irvin Heitzenrater, he was born
      Aug. 1, 1908 (MC).

MILES JAY-10 DORMIRE, b. Oct. 13, 1916 (MC);
   d.
   m. June 8, 1948 Ruby Harbert (MC); they are now divorced(MC).

****

WILLIAM CLARK-9 CROASMUN (Miles-8, Asa-7, Asa-6,
                          James-5, Joseph-4, Joseph-3,
                          Robert-2, John-1)

b. Feb. 3, 1876 (MC);
d. Jan. 16, 1959 (MC);
m(1). June 22, 1904 Clara Grace Gilmore, "Polly" was born
      May 24, 1889 (MC); they divorced (MC);
m(2). Dec. 22, 1920 Sara Elizabeth "Sophie" Martin, she
      was born Feb. 18, 1884 and died Sept. 13, 1971 (MC).

   CHILDREN:

ELVIRA FAY-10 CROASMUN, b. May 22, 1905 (MC);
     d. Sept. 18, 1906 (MC); died at 16 months (MC).

see page
569
MILDRED JANE-10 CROASMUN, b. Aug. 3, 1907 (MC);
     d.
     m.   James Monroe Whitaker, born Feb.6,1900(MC).

see page
570
HELEN OLIVE-10 CROASMUN, b. Feb. 10, 1912 (MC);
     d.
     m. Dec. 16,1931 Paul N. Lusk, born Jan. 10, 1909 (MC).

MARGARET LOUISE-10 CROASMUN, b. Dec.28, 1921 (MC);
     d.
     m. June 15, 1946 Steven Richard Petho, born June 14,1923(MC).
     Children:
       BARBARA LESLIE-11 PETHO, b. March 19, 1947 (MC).
       SANDRA IRENE-11 PETHO, b. Sept. 28, 1949 (MC).
       STEVEN RICHARD-11 PETHO, b. March 31, 1954 (MC).
       DAVID EUGENE-11 PETHO, b. Jan. 1, 1958 (MC).
       RONALD CLARK-11 PETHO, b. Dec. 28, 1961 (MC).

DAVID CLARK-10 CROASMUN, b. July 10, 1925 (MC).
     d. April 20, 1945 (MC); killed in Germany during World
     War II (MC).

****

see page
507

NATHAN BURTON-9 CROASMUN (Miles-8, Asa-7, Asa-6,
James-5, Joseph-4, Joseph-3,
Robert-2, John-1)
b. Jan. 3, 1879, twin (MC);
d. Dec. 20, 1964 (MC);
m. Dec. 17, 1908 Belva Jane Blakely, she was born Oct. 23,
1884 and she died June 2, 1973 (MC).
CHILDREN:

see page
571

<u>NELLIE JANE-10 CROASMUN</u>, b. Sept. 16, 1911 (MC);
d.
m. Sept. 19, 1928 Wilbur Leroy Sheesley, he was born
March 23, 1907 (MC).

RALPH BLAKELY-10 CROASMUN, b. Sept. 12, 1916 (MC);
d.
m. Oct. 18, 1939 Janette Emerick, born May 30,1922(MC);
they divorced (MC).
m(2). Jan. 10, 1954 Edith Hathaway, she was born Nov.
17, 1916 and died June 25, 1965 (MC).
Children:
LINDA DARLENE-11 CROASMUN, b. Oct. 10, 1947 (MC);
m.Dec.14,1968 Gordon R. Usrey (MC).

BURTON RAY-10 CROASMUN, b. Oct. 27, 1920 (MC);
d.
m. June 28, 1941 Fanny Idessa Elder (MC).
m(2).Oct.20,1956 Ann Wineberg (MC).
Children:
SUSAN ELAINE-11 CROASMUN, b. March 25, 1949 (MC).
SALLY ANN-11 CROASMUN, b. March 28, 1952 (MC).
JAN LYNN-11 CROASMUN, b. Nov. 28,1957 (MC).
JERRY RAY-11 CROASMUN, b. May 13, 1959 (MC).

JOHN LEHR-10 CROASMUN, b. July 4, 1923 (MC);
d. Oct. 31, 1923 in infancy (MC).

****

see page
508

DANIEL HENRY-9 CROASMUN (James-8, Asa-7, Asa-6, James-5, Joseph-4, Joseph-3, Robert-2, John-1)

b. June 28, 1866, twin (MC);
d. July 5, 1946 (MC);
m. Oct. 8, 1886 Effie Margaret Mauk, she was born Nov. 28, 1868 and died Nov. 15, 1944 (MC).

CHILDREN:

see page
572
LULA ALICE-10 CROASMUN, b. Dec.16,1887 (MC);
    d.July 26, 1967 (MC);
    m.Feb.10,1908 Saul Johnson,b.April 2,1886, d. 1975(MC).

see page
573
HOMER BURR-10 CROASMUN, b. Jan.31,1890 (MC);
    d.Jan. 31, 1976 (MC);
    m.April 21,1917 Alma Johnston, b.Feb.28,1892 (MC).

OTIS HUGH-10 CROASMUN, b.July 15, 1892 (MC);
    m.July 2,1914 Virginia "Vinnie" Smathers,b.March 23,1894(MC).
    Children:
        MARIAN CORINNE-11 CROASMUN,b.March 9,1917 (MC);
            d.March 23,1941 (MC); m.March 1939 Jack Smith (MC).

see page
574
SIDNEY-10 CROASMUN, b.Jan.17,1894 (MC);
    m.Oct.16,1915 Inez Smathers, b. March 8,1892 (MC).

NATHAN CLARK-10 CROASMUN, b.March 9, 1896 (MC);
    m.(1)   Elizabeth Harris, they divorced (MC);
    m.(2)   Frances Bronhauser (MC);
    m.(3)Jan.29, 1954 Edith Marie Dennison, d.Jan. 1973 (MC).

JAMES JACOB "Jay"-10 CROASMUN,b.Aug.5,1902 (MC);
    d.April 29,1945(MC);
    m.Sept.29,1929 Louise Henthorn, b.Nov.9,1909 (MC).
    Children:
        WALTER JAMES-11 CROASMUN, b.Sept.19,1930(MC).
        HENRY-11 CROASMUN, b. March 20, 1934 (MC).
        KAREN-11 CROASMUN, b. Sept.   , 1944 (MC).

see page
575
GERALDINE MARSH-10 CROASMUN, b.March 30,1904 (MC);
    m.Aug.23,1923 George Plowman, b.June 21,1902 (MC).

see page
576
ROBERT FRANK-10 CROASMUN, b.Oct. 1, 1906 (MC);
    m(1).Jan.   ,1932 Dorothy Famous, they divorced (MC);
    m(2).Aug.17,1933 Gertrude McHoffie, b.July 28,1907(MC).

see page
577
MARGARET ISABEL-10 CROASMUN, b.Nov.9,1908 (MC);
    m.Sept. 27,1927 Charles Otto Neal,b.Nov.27,1901 and he
        died Oct. 16, 1963 (MC).

see page
578
DONALD HENRY "Pete"-10 CROASMUN, b.May 16, 1912 (MC);
    d.Nov. 25, 1977 (MC);
    m.June 15, 1932 Katheryn Jane Kuntz, b.Feb.11,1915(MC).

****

HARRY NEWTON-9 CHAMBERS   (Elizabeth-8, Asa-7, Asa-6,
                          James-5, Joseph-4, Joseph-3,
                          Robert-2, John-1)
b. Dec. 5, 1867 (MC);
d.   1941 (MC);
m. Nov. 28, 1895 Mary Olive Sprankle, she was born Feb.
   7, 1873 and died Jan. of 1963 (MC).

    CHILDREN:

JAMES KARL-10 CHAMBERS, b. Jan. 3, 1898 (MC);
    d. June 30, 1972 (MC);
    m. Dec. 28, 1917 Anna Viola Martin,b.Aug.25,1901(MC);
    m(2) Catherine Deer (MC).
    lived at New Castle, PA (MC).
    Children: (al by first marriage)
       INFANT-11 CHAMBERS, b.   ; d.____ (MC).
       OLIVE JANE-11 CHAMBERS, b.Oct.26,1920 (MC);
          m.William Tarr (MC); lived at Butler, PA (MC).
       FREDERICK LEE-11 CHAMBERS, b. Feb. 9, 1924 (MC);
          lived at Trade City, PA (MC).
WILLIAM DEAN-10 CHAMBERS, b. Dec. 5, 1901 (MC);
    m.April 21,1923 Beulah Frew, b.June 25,1902 (MC);
    lived at Butler, PA (MC).
    Children:
       BETTY IRENE-11 CHAMBERS, b. Jan. 15, 1924 (MC).
       IMOGENE GRACE-11 CHAMBERS, b. May 9, 1927 (MC).
SHARRETS SPRANKLE-10 CHAMBERS, b. Dec. 22, 1904 (MC);
    m. June 15, 1926 Etta Knauf, b.June 16, 1906 (MC).
    m(2)________________(MC); lived at Beaver, PA (MC).
    Children: (all by first marriage)
       SHARRETS-11 CHAMBERS, b. May 14, 1928 (MC).
       CLIFFORD CHARLES-11 CHAMBERS, b. Jan. 20, 1931(MC).
HAROLD-10 CHAMBERS, b. May 24, 1913 (MC);
    d. April 10, 1914 in infancy (MC).

                ****

see page
509

ANNA DORA-9 CHAMBERS (Elizabeth-8, Asa-7, Asa-6,
                James-5, Joseph-4, Joseph-3,
                Robert-2, John-1)
b. April 5, 1868 (MC);
d. Sept. 1939 (MC);
m. Anna Dora Chambers never married (MC).

    CHILDREN:

ADELBERT DANKS-10 CHAMBERS, b. Nov. 27, 1899 (MC);
    d.
    m. June 29, 1920 Mary Knauf (MC).
    Children:
        DOROTHY JANE-11 CHAMBERS, b.   ; d. at one week (MC).
        ANNA DORIS-11 CHAMBERS, b. May 15, 1922 (MC).
        ETHEL PAULINE-11 CHAMBERS, b. Jan. 13, 1924 (MC).
        MARIE "Mellie"-11 CHAMBERS, b. Feb. 1, 1926 (MC).
        MARY ELIZABETH-11 CHAMBERS, b. June 13, 1929 (MC).

                ****

Genealogy of the Crossman Family, Supplement #3 • ©1990 by Robert Owen Crossman • 908 Front • Conway, AR 72032

see page
509

ZIELA BLANCHE-9 CHAMBERS   (Elizabeth-8, Asa-7, Asa-6,
                    James-5, Joseph-4, Joseph-3,
                    Robert-2, John-1)
  b. Sept. 17, 1875, twin (MC);
  d. Sept.   1957 (MC);
  m. Sept. 17, 1903 Harvey Jacob Dormire, he was born on
      Jan. 29, 1879 and he disappeared with no record in
      1931 or 1932 (MC).

      CHILDREN:

  JAMES MAX-10 DORMIRE, b. Jan. 21, 1904 (MC);
      d. Feb.11,1968 William Cemetery, White Bluff, Tenn.(MC);
      m. July 5, 1935 Charlotte Travis, b.Nov.19,1906(MC).
  HARVEY JACOB-10 DORMIRE, Jr., b.   1906 (MC);
      d. in infancy (MC).

see page
579

  MARTHA ELIZABETH-10 DORMIRE, b. May 9, 1910 (MC);
      d.   ; lived in Claipbury, PA (MC).
      m. July 8, 1933 Herbert Ross Wees., he was born April
          23, 1901 and died March 9, 1966 (MC).
  MABEL INEZ-10 DORMIRE, b. July 9, 1915 (MC);
      m. June 11, 1938 Archie M. Means, b.March 4,1918(MC);
      lived in Sheffield, PA.
      Children:
        SUZANNA-11 MEANS, b. June 17, 1940 (MC);
          m. Jan. 2, 1960 Thomas McNeal (MC).
          Children:
            STACY ANN-12 McNEAL, b. April 17, 1963 (MC).
            STEPHEN-12 McNEAL, b. Oct. 31, 1967 (MC).
        HERBERT WARREN-11 MEANS, b. Aug. 29, 1949 (MC).

                ****

see page
509

MILES BLANCHARD-9 CHAMBERS (Elizabeth-8, Asa-7, Asa-6,
                            James-5, Joseph-4, Joseph-3,
                            Robert-2, John-1)
b. Sept. 17, 1875 (MC);
d. April   1954 (MC);
m.   Carrie Dorothea Jordon, she was born
    on May 21, 1878 and died May 15, 1972 (MC).

    CHILDREN:

CATHERINE GRACE-10 CHAMBERS, b. March 3, 1899 (MC);
    d.   1963 (MC);
    m. July 2, 1928 Charles Patrick Couse, b.May 16,1899(MC).
    Children:

        CATHERINE JORDON-11 COUSE, b. Aug. 31, 1929 (MC).

        JAMES PATRICK-11 COUSE, b. Jan. 16, 1933 (MC).

        MONA GRACE-11 COUSE, b. Dec. 2, 1939 (MC).

JAMES LAIRD-10 CHAMBERS, b. April 28, 1902 (MC);
    d. May 16, 1968 (MC);
    m. Aug. 23, 1958 Sara Beele William Travis (MC).

                ****

see page
509

ETHEL MARGRETTA-9 CHAMBERS (Elizabeth-8, Asa-7, Asa-6,
                        James-5, Joseph-4, Joseph-3,
                        Robert-2, John-1)
b. March 29, 1879 (MC);
d. June 20, 1956 (MC);
m. May 1, 1900 William Sheridan Shaffer, he was born on
   Sept. 5, 1871 and died May 17, 1956 (MC).

   CHILDREN:.

ANNA MARIE-10 SHAFFER, b. Aug. 27, 1900 (MC);
   d.   ; Anna was an Registered Nurse.(MC);
   m. Oct. 7, 1944 Howard L. Merritt, he was born March
      21,1898 and died Jan.24,1963 (MC).

see page
580

FRANK ROOSEVELT-10 SHAFFER, b. Jan. 13, 1902 (MC);
   d.   ; all children by first marriage(MC);
   m(1)Oct.15,1924 Myrtle Vivienne Gabrielson, she was
      born June 17,1905 and died Aug.5,1956 (MC);
   m(2)Aug.23,1958 Verna Krantz, b.April 6,1907 (MC).

see page
581

ELIZABETH JANE-10 SHAFFER, b. Aug. 5, 1914 (MC);
   m. June 26, 1937 Frederick Lott Oliver Griffith, he
      was born Feb.24,1908 and died July 2,1967 (MC).

DWIGHT SHERIDAN-10 SHAFFER, b. June 1, 1918 (MC);
   d. March 10, 1972 (MC);
   m. Dec.30,1939 Irma Mastrian, b.March 14,1918 (MC).
   Children:
      JUDITH ANN-11 SHAFFER, b.April 6, 1941 (MC);
         m. Feb. 6, 1960 Anthony Cafaro, b.April 26,1937(MC).
         Children:
            JANICE ANN-12 CAFARO, b.Nov.13,1961 (MC).
      JOHN SHERIDAN-11 SHAFFER, b. Feb. 24, 1948 (MC).

      MICHAEL PHILIP-11 SHAFFER, b. Nov. 28, 1953 (MC).

JAMES WILLIAM-10 SHAFFER, b.May 19,1920 (MC);
   d.Jan. 27, 1963 (MC);
   m. June 5, 1948 Sarah Jane Lukehart, b.Nov.20,1920(MC).

****

Genealogy of the Crossman Family, Supplement #3 • ©1990 by Robert Owen Crossman • 908 Front • Conway, AR 72032

JAMES ASA GARFIELD-9 CHAMBERS (Elizabeth-8,Asa-7,Asa-6,
James-5, Joseph-4, Joseph-3,
Robert-2, John-1)
b. Jan.31,1881(MC);
d. April 24, 1932 (MC);
m. Dec. 18, 1909 Mabel Etta McConaughty, she was born on
July 30,1889 and died Dec. 8, 1947 (MC).

CHILDREN:

DONALD BROOKS-10 CHAMBERS, b. July 19, 1912 (MC);
d.Jan.14,1971 Round Top Cemetery, Pux......., PA (MC);
m.Nov.3,1935 or Nov.4,1934 Mary Evelyn Broscius (MC).
Children:
BETTY-11 CHAMBERS, b.Dec.20,1934 (MC);
m.Joseph L. Heberman (MC).
Children:
JOSEPH LEROY-12 HEBERMAN, b.March 19,1956(MC).
PAUL ALAN-12 HEBERMAN, b.Oct. 2,1958 (MC).
LISA ANN-12 HEBERMAN, b. March 16, 1966 (MC).
THELMA-11 CHAMBERS,b.June 7,1931(MC);m.___Hyskell(MC).
DONALD-11 CHAMBERS,b.Sept.2,1941(MC);m.Shirley___(MC).
NORMAN-11 CHAMBERS,b.April 10,1944 (MC).
BONNIE JEAN-11 CHAMBERS,b.March 21,1946(MC);m.__Fisher(MC).
ROBERT-11 CHAMBERS, b. March 8, 1947 (MC).
MARY LaRUE-10 CHAMBERS, b.Oct.21,1915 (MC);
m.June 10,1939 Wayne Reid Smith (MC).
Children:
JOANNE-11 SMITH, b.   (MC).
DENNIS-11 SMITH, b.   (MC).
DAVID-11 SMITH, b.   (MC).
MARGARET IONE-10 CHAMBERS, b.March 29, 1919 (MC);
m.Nov.18,1941 Ralph Roy Young, b.April 6,1919 (MC).
Children:
RALPH RONALD-11 YOUNG,b.Feb.7,1943 (MC);
m.April 18,1964 Cheryl Ann Fagley, b.Dec.6,1944(MC).
Children:
RONALD KEVIN-12 YOUNG, b.Jan.29,1965 (MC).
DAVID MERLE-12 YOUNG, b. April 6, 1967 (MC).
RICHARD GARFIELD-11 YOUNG, b.Nov.12,1946 (MC);
m.Nov.12,1966 Barbara Lynn Laughlin,b.Jan.20,1951(MC).
Children:
JENNIFER LYNN-12 YOUNG, b. June 1, 1967 (MC).
RODNEY LEE-11 YOUNG, b.March 18, 1949 (MC).
TERRY HAROLD-11 YOUNG, b. March 12, 1951 (MC).
SHEILA IONE-11 YOUNG, b.Nov. 22, 1948 (? MC).
WAYNE CLYDE-10 CHAMBERS, b. April 21, 1921 (MC);
m.Oct.15,1948 Arline Norma Sands (MC).
Children:
DOLORES ARLINE-11 CHAMBERS, b. Aug. 8, 1935 (MC);
step child of Wayne (MC).
KATHY LYNN-11 CHAMBERS, b. Oct. 8, 1949 (MC).

****

538

see page
509

AUGUSTA MAUD-9 CHAMBERS (Elizabeth-8, Asa-7, Asa-6, **James-5, Joseph-4, Joseph-3, Robert-2, John-1)**

b. Nov. 10, 1885 (MC);
d. still living in 1978 (MC);
m. May 11, 1910 Edward Lee Fleming, he was a Doctor, born
on Sept. 21, 1884 and died______(MC).

CHILDREN:

MILDRED JOSEPHINE-10 FLEMING, b.April 19, 1911 (MC);
d. May 18, 1912 died in infancy (MC).

HELEN RUTH-10 FLEMING, b. Feb. 20, 1913 (MC);
m(1)   (MC);
m(2)May 18,1958 Albert Logan Miller, b.Jan.17,1911(MC).

LILLIAN PAULINE-10 FLEMING, b. Dec. 1, 1916 (MC);
m. Aug. 7, 1940 Harry F. Schmidt, b.Aug.3,1915 (MC).
Children:
EDWARD LEE-11 SCHMIDT, b. May 31, 1947 (MC).

HARRY CHARLES-11 SCHMIDT, b. Sept. 1, 1948 (MC).

EDWARD LEE-10 FLEMING, Jr., b.Dec.30,1918 (MC);
m. June Hall (MC).
Children:
ROBERT MICHAEL-11 FLEMING, b.   (MC).
DOUGLAS LEE-11 FLEMING, b.   (MC).
MARY LOU-11 FLEMING, b.   (MC).
JOHN CRAIG-11 FLEMING, b.   (MC).

ELENOR JANE-10 FLEMING, b. April 27, 1923 (MC);
m. Fred Meshler, Jr.
Children:
DAVID ANTHONY-11 MESHLER, b.   (MC).
PATRICIA JANE-11 MESHLER, b.   (MC).

****

This page is intentionally blank
to allow the next generation
to begin on a right hand page.

Our
Tenth
Generation

ALFRED MONROE-10 DENMAN (Esther-9, William-8, Rebecca-7,
                         Asa-6, James-5, Joseph-4, Joseph-3,
                         Robert-2, John-1)
b. July 18, 1892 at Denman home, 3 miles north of Hillyard,
   Washington (AD); 'attended Hillyard schools'(AD);
d. living in Spokane, Washington in 1977;
m. 1914 Lillie Rose (AD) or Lily Rose (AD).

   CHILDREN:

ELLEN ESTHER-11 DENMAN, b.1915 "at old home"(AD);
   d.
   m.   Al Harris (AD); have three sons (AD).

MONROE C.-11 DENMAN, b. 1916 at Molson, Wash. (AD);
   d.
   m. Eileen Keller and has three children (AD).

MARY MARGARET-11 DENMAN, b. 1922 at Old Home (AD);
   d.
   m. Lester M. Leamer and has three children (AD).

BESSIE MAY-11 DENMAN, b. 1923 at Old Home (AD);
   d.
   m. Robert Mott and has three children (AD).

IRENE EVELYN-11 DENMAN, b. 1927 at home (AD);
   d.
   m. Robert Dotson (AD).

The following was written to me in a letter dated Sept. 4,
1977 by Alfred M. Denman who is the author of all the
information followed by the initials AD.
   "I left home with horses and covered wagon on Dec. 5,
1913 for a new home making the 200 odd miles in 8 days
near Molson, Wahington. It was equipted with log buildings,
a well in the barnyard, about 40 acres plowed with lots of
willows cut off above ground and about 40 big trees on the
field so spent a lot of time clearing the field while
putting in my crops. I soon found it froze every month
in the year so couldn't raise any garden and almost no
flowers. But found many beautiful flowers in the woods
or timber that was a beautiful second growth of timber.
My wife was an English girl and I wondered a good many
times how she could stand the Frontier living but we
many times said it was the high light of our lives. We
were here for 6½ years and had to leave as we had no way
of getting our daughter and son to school. We lived in
a high valley that was above the little town and 2 miles
by road."
   "Our children are of course all married and most of
the grandchildren also. I am 85 years old and have had
to sell the farm and move into a trailer-house which is
luckily on the back of daughter Ellen Harris's acre.
Have quit driving so have to ask for help often."
   "This trip by covered wagon in a way prepared me to
write out the trip of ASA and PATIENCE, knowing that the
days trip by oxen was about 12 miles at most, loaded as
they were."

see page
513

JESSIE WILLIAM "J.W."-10 HICKS   (Elizabeth-9, Mary-8, Asa-7,
Asa-6, James-5, Joseph-4, Joseph-3,
Robert-2, John-1)

b. Oct. 22, 1878 (MC);
d.
m.(1) Lana Postewaite, she was born Oct. 27, 1876 and
      she died in 1902 (MC);
m.(2) Sarah Elizabeth Neil (MC).

CHILDREN (by first marriage):

JOSEPH ROY-11 HICKS, b.April 2, 1903 (MC);
     d. Aug. 13, 1905 (MC); died in childhood (MC).

see page
588 ABRAM RALPH-11 HICKS, b. May 18, 1908 (MC);
     d.
     m. March 2, 1928 Mildred Emma Crawford (MC).

see page
589 WILLIAM RAY-11 HICKS, b. March 27, 1907 (MC);
     d.
     m. June 16, 1935 Marjorie Emma Andrews (MC).

see page
590 RUTH MAE-11 HICKS, b. April 25, 1909 (MC);
     d.
     m. Aug. 28, 1930 William Floyd Hoover (MC).

CHILDREN (by second marriage):

VERA JEANNETTE-11 HICKS, b. Aug.15,1918 (MC);
     d.
     m. Sept. 27, 1939 Wayne Kister Stiteler (MC).
     CHILDREN:

          NANCY ANN-12 STITELER, b. July 1, 1941 (MC).

          LOIS REA-12 STITELER, b. June 23, 1946 (MC).

LAURA LUCILE-11 HICKS, b.Oct.29,1920 (MC);
     d.
     m. June 23, 1942 William B. Lawrence (MC).

     CHILDREN:

          SALLY LYNN-12 LAWRENCE, b. June 26, 1946 (MC).

          GEORGE WILLIAMS-12 LAWRENCE, b. July 16,1947(MC).

Genealogy of the Crossman Family, Supplement #3 · ©1990 by Robert Owen Crossman · 908 Front · Conway, AR 72032

see page
513

MARY ADDA VERNA "Verna Marie" HICKS (Elizabeth-9, Mary-8,
              Asa-7, Asa-6, James-5, Joseph-4, Joseph-3,
                          Robert-2, John-1)

     b. Nov. 23, 1880 (MC);
     d.
     m. Dec.   1906 David Anthony Gross, he died June
        13, 1929 (MC).

     CHILDREN:
ANNA E.-11 GROSS, b.June 14,   (MC);
   d.
   m. James Hurlock (MC).

DAVID ANTHONY-11 GROSS, Jr., b.Nov.20,   (MC);
   d.
   m. Vada Woohall (MC).

RUTH JANE-11 GROSS, b. May 1,   (MC);
   d.
   m. Russell Clemo (MC).

GEORGE EDWARD-11 GROSS, b.April 1, 1911 (MC).
   d.
   m.

BOYD G.-11 GROSS, b.
   d.
   m. Velma Crisco (MC).
      CHILDREN:
        MARK NOEL-12 GROSS,b.   (MC).
        BETTY-12 GROSS, b.   m.Paul Strong (MC).
        DIAN-12 GROSS, b.   (MC).
        JACKIE-12 GROSS, b. (MC).

MARY IRENE-11 GROSS, b.
   d.
   m.

HELEN KATHERINE-11 GROSS, b.Sept.10,1912 (MC);
   d.
   m. John Williams (MC).

JOSEPH A.-11 GROSS, b.
   d.
   m.

RICHARD F.-11 GROSS, b.
   d.
   m. Jeanie Erskin (MC).
      CHILDREN:
        CAROL JEANIE-12 GROSS, b.   (MC).

****

PRESTON BARRACK-10 HICKS   (Elizabeth-9, Mary-8, Asa-7, Asa-6,
                             James-5, Joseph-4, Joseph-3,
                             Robert-2, John-1)

b. Oct. 30, 1884 (MC);
d.
m. Dollie L. Lamison (MC).

   CHILDREN:

GLENN PAUL-11 HICKS, b.
   d.
   m. Ruth Hines (MC).

CECILANNA-11 HICKS, b.
   d.
   m. Frank L. Lewis (MC). They had five children.
      CHILDREN:
         JUDITH ANN-12 LEWIS, b.   (MC).
            d.
            m.

         THOMAS JOSEPH-12 LEWIS, b.   (MC).
            d.
            m.

         JOHN MEAD-12 HICKS, b.   (MC).
            d.
            m.

         MERLE MAX-12 HICKS, b.   (MC).
            d.
            m.

         WARREN EARL-12 HICKS, b.   (MC).
            d.
            m.

              ****

Genealogy of the Crossman Family, Supplement #3 · ©1990 by Robert Owen Crossman · 908 Front · Conway, AR 72032

LUCRIETIA MAUD-10 HICKS   (Elizabeth-9, Mary-8, Asa-7, Asa-6.
                             James-5, Joseph-4, Joseph-3,
                             Robert-2, John-1)
    b. Nov. 23, 1886 (MC);
    d.
    m. Feb. 4, 1907 John Gourly Crawford, he was born
       March 8, 1884 (MC).

      CHILDREN:

VAUGH HICKS-11 CRAWFORD, b. Aug.27,1907 (MC);
    d.
    m. July 15, 1930 Vivian Carr, she was born May 12,1910(MC).
      CHILDREN:
        ROBERT EUGENE-12 CRAWFORD, b.May 16,1931 (MC).
        HELEN MARIE-12 CRAWFORD, b. 1936 (MC).
        RUTH ANN-12 CRAWFORD, b. 1937 (MC).
        JOSEPH-12 CRAWFORD, b. 1945 (MC).

HELEN ROSANNA-11 CRAWFORD, b.June 15, 1909 (MC);
    d.
    m. May 15, 1928 Carl L. Ferringer, he was born Nov.4,1909(MC).
      CHILDREN:
        FLORENCE LOUISE-12 FERRINGER, b.Nov.20,1928(MC);
         m. John Hozlett (MC).
        PAUL WILSON-12 FERRINGER, b. Sept. 10, 1930 (MC).
        DONALD.CARL-12 FERRINGER, b. March 12, 1932 (MC).
        MARJORIE LUCRETIA-12 FERRINGER,b.June 17,1934(MC).
        MARION RUTH-12 FERRINGER, b. 1936 (MC).
        HELEN MAXINE-12 FERRINGER, b. 1942 (MC).

WALTER GOURLY-11 CRAWFORD, b. Feb. 11, 1911 (MC);
    d.
    m. Vivian Gass (MC).
      CHILDREN:
        DARRELL JOHN-12 CRAWFORD, b.1943 (MC).
        JOYCE ANN-12 CRAWFORD, b. 1945 (MC).

MARION MABEL-11 CRAWFORD, b.Aug.31,1912 (MC);
    d. May 19, 1914 in childhood (MC).

MARTHA RUTH-11 CRAWFORD, b.Dec. 29, 1913 (MC);
    d.
    m. Jack P. Boyd (MC).
      CHILDREN:
        D. ELAINE-12 BOYD, b. 1946 (MC).

DAVID CLARK-11 CRAWFORD, b.Dec. 31, 1914 (MC);
    d.
    m. Cora Ann Weaver (MC).
      CHILDREN:
        CAROL ANN-12 CRAWFORD, b. 1941 (MC).
        SANDRA KAY-12 CRAWFORD, b. 1944 (MC).

continued

see page
544

LUCRIETIA MAUD-10 HICKS continued.

    CHILDREN:

WILLIAM HUGH-11 CRAWFORD, b. July 15, 1916 (MC);
    d.
    m. Frances Strickland (MC). They had three children.
        CHILDREN:
            BEVERLY ANN-12 CRAWFORD, b. 1938 (MC).
            KAREN LEE-12 CRAWFORD, b. 1941 (MC).
            WILLIAM CLARK-12 CRAWFORD, b. 1943 (MC).

JOHN GOURLY-11 CRAWFORD, Jr., b. Nov. 11, 1917 (MC);
    d.
    m. Margaret Smith (MC).
        CHILDREN:
            THOMAS PATRICK-12 CRAWFORD, b. 1946 (MC).

VIANA MARIE-11 CRAWFORD, b. Nov.3, 1919 (MC);
    d.
    m. Joseph Halchin (MC).

ELIZABETH ANN "Betty"-11 CRAWFORD, b.March 18,1924 (MC);
    d.
    m. Ralph Henry (MC).
        CHILDREN:
            GARY ERVIN-12 HENRY, b. 1948 (MC).

ERNIE MARGARET-10 HICKS (Elizabeth-9, Mary-8, Asa-7, Asa-6,
                    James-5, Joseph-4, Joseph-3,
                    Robert-2, John-1)

        b. July 7, 1894 (MC);
        d.
        m. John Myers (MC).

        CHILDREN;

   ROBERT BARRACK-11 MEYERS, b. June 13, 1921 (MC);
      d.
    m. Jean Waterson (MC).
        CHILDREN:
            JAMES CHRISTOPHER-12 MYERS, b.   (MC).
            TIMOTHY ROBERT-12 MYERS, b.   (MC).

MARY M.-10 HARWICK   (Matilda-9, Mary-8, Asa-7, Asa-6,
                          James-5, Joseph-4, Joseph-3,
     b. Oct. 7, 1877 (MC);   Robert-2, John-1)
     d. Feb. 12, 1904 (MC);
     m. July 8, 1897 W. Edward Heitzenrater (MC).

     CHILDREN:

PAUL-11 HEITZENRATER, b.Nov. 20, 1897 (MC);
     d. Dec. 28, 1918 (MC).

IRENE-11 HEITZENRATER, b. Dec. 5, 1898 (MC);
     d.
     m. Kennedy (MC).

WILLIAM-11 HEITZENRATER, b. July 12, 1900 (MC);
     d.

****

MELISSA GERTRUDE-10 HARWICK   (Matilda-9, Mary-8, Asa-7, Asa-6,
                                    James-5, Joseph-4, Joseph-3,
                                    Robert-2, John-1)

      b. July 8, 1879 (MC);
      d. Feb. 26, 1904 (MC);
      m. Jan. 17, 1902 M______ Depp (MC).

            CHILDREN:

see page
592 CARMEN E.-11 DEPP, b. Nov.20,1899 (MC);
            d.
            m. Nov. 9, 1919 George Sprankle, he was born in 1898
               and died in 1960 (MC).

      DWIGHT-11 DEPP, b. Aug. 20, 1903 (MC);
            d. Sept. 6, 1922 in youth (MC).

                    ****

see page
514

JAMES J.-10 HARWICK   (Matilda-9, Mary-8, Asa-7, Asa-6,
                        James-5, Joseph-4, Joseph-3,
                        Robert-2, John-1)
b. Sept. 19, 1881 (MC);
d.
m. April 27, 1907 Eva "Mae Nie" Lydic (MC).
    CHILDREN:

ELMER EDWIN-11 HARWICK, b.Aug.6,1901 (MC);
    d.
    m. Elma Sue Roberts Brooks (MC).
       CHILDREN:
          ELMER EDWIN-12 HARWICK jr.,b.May 13,1942 (MC);
            m. Nancy Honcie Gilley (MC).
          JAMES ERNEST-12 HARWICK, b.Aug.27,1947 (MC).
          NANCY MAE JANE-12 HARWICK, b.Dec.10,1948 (MC).

LUELLA BERNICE-11 HARWICK, b.Feb.23,1911 (MC);
    d.
    m. Burr James Sprankle (MC).
       CHILDREN:
          BURR EDWARD-12 SPRANKLE, b.April 17,1929 (MC);
            m. Meredith Ludwig (MC).
          ANDREW LEROY-12 SPRANKLE, b.Nov.15,1930 (MC);
            m. Patricia Maer (MC).
          PATRICIA MAE-12 SPRANKLE, b.Aug.7,1932 (MC).

JAMES ANDREW-11 HARWICK, b. Feb.6,1913 (MC);
    d.April 16,1913 in infancy (MC).

CLAUDE ROBERT-11 HARWICK, b.April 17,1914 (MC);
    d.
    m. Virgil ? Hill (MC).
       CHILDREN:
          JOAN-12 HARWICK, b. Aug.27,1935 (MC).

MICHAEL GEORGE-11 HARWICK, b.Jan.28,1920 (MC);
    d.
    m. Emily Marie Bonessa (MC).

ALBERT WILLIAM-11 HARWICK, b.
    d.
    m. Esther Elizabeth Kroh ? (MC).
       CHILDREN:
          JAMES PAUL-12 HARWICK, b. Jan.17,1947 (MC).
          ALBERT WILLIAM-12 HARWICK Jr., b.Jan.15,1948 (MC).

****

ALBERT BARTON-10 HARWICK   (Matilda-9, Mary-8, Asa-7, Asa-6,
                                James-5, Joseph-4, Joseph-3,
                                Robert-2, John-1)

b. July 19, 1886 (MC);
d. July 22, 1964 (MC);
m. July 4, 1906 Myrtle Bush, she was born March 15, 1889,
   and was interviewed by Marion Croasmun on Sept.7,1977(MC).

   CHILDREN:

MAX C.-11 HARWICK, b.March 23,1907 (MC);
   d.
   m.Sept.9,1928 Mary Geraldine Williamson, born Oct.13,1906(MC).
      CHILDREN:
         JOHN CLINTON-HARWICK, b.Nov.33,1932 (MC);
            m. Mary Carolyn Myers (MC).
               CHILDREN:
                  BARRY-13 HARWICK, b.1955 (MC).
                  ROBERT-13 HARWICK, b. July 3, 1956 (MC).
                  MARY BETH-13 HARWICK, b.July 26,1957 (MC).
         MARY LOU-12 HARWICK, b. March 1936 (MC);
            m. Kenneth McJunkin (MC).
               CHILDREN:
                  JAMES-13 McJUNKIN, b.Nov.20,1961 (MC).
                  KEVIN-13 McJUNKIN, b.Sept.19,1966 (MC).
         PATRICIA LEE-12 HARWICK, b. May   1939 (MC);
            d. Walter Carmo (MC).
               CHILDREN:
                  GERRI LYNN-13 CARMO, b. Aug.7,1962 (MC).
                  ROBBIE-13 CARMO, b. Dec.19,1969 (MC).

BEULAH B.-11 HARWICK, b. Feb.10,1909 (MC);
   d.
   m. Earl Johns, he was born in 1912 (MC);   they divorced(MC).

see page
516

WILLIAM CLARK-10 CROSSMAN (George-9, Isaac-8, Asa-7, Asa-6,
                        James-5, Joseph-4, Joseph-3,
                        Robert-2, John-1)

b. Dec. 14, 1894 (MC)
d.
m. Feb. 20, 1926 Mary Holliman, she was born April 11,
   1905 (MC). They live at Vienna, Virginia (MC).

   CHILDREN:

WILLIAM CLARK-11 CROSSMAN, b. Dec. 14, 1926 (MC);
   m.Feb.20,19__ Elizabeth Jane "Pat" Cleer, she was born
      Oct. 8, 1926 (MC).
   Children:
      WILLIAM CLARK-12 CROSSMAN, b.Aug.12,1946 (MC).
      SANDRA SUE-12 CROSSMAN, b.Aug.2,1948 (MC);
        m.Aug.12,1967 William Roger Kelley (MC).
        Children:
           CHRISTOPHER CROSSMAN-13 KELLEY, b.Dec.19,1968(MC).
           ANDREW CROSSMAN-13 KELLEY, b.Feb.26,1970 (MC).
      GEORGE GRANT-12 CROSSMAN, b.Sept.12,1949 (MC).
      JUDITH COLLEEN-12 CROSSMAN, b.Jan.2,1951 (MC);
        m. Alan Wayne Everhart (MC).
        Children:
           SAMATHA E.-13 EVERHART, b.   (MC).
           ALAN WAYNE-13 EVERHART, b.   (MC).
      PAMELA CAROL-12 CROSSMAN, b. Jan. 12, 1955 (MC).
      OTIS CHARLES-12 CROSSMAN, b. May 31, 1956 (MC).

VIRGINIA MARIE-11 CROSSMAN, b.May 7, 1930 (MC);
   m. July 9, 1949 R. Harrison Groves, he was born June
      28, 1925 (MC).

   Children:

      SHARON LANE-12 GROVES, b. Sept. 30, 1951 (MC);
        m. 1977__________(MC).

      RANDOLPH HARRISON-12 GROVES, b. April 19, 1954 (MC).

      CLAYTON DODGE-12 GROVES, b. March 18, 1957 (MC).

      STEPHEN GRANT-12 GROVES, b. Aug. 25, 1961 (MC).

****

Genealogy of the Crossman Family, Supplement #3 • ©1990 by Robert Owen Crossman • 908 Front • Conway, AR 72032

see page
516

FLORENCE CELESTE-10 CROSSMAN (George-9, Isaac-8, Asa-7, Asa-6,
                    James-5, Joseph-4, Joseph-3,
                    Robert-2, John-1)

b. Nov. 24, 1897 (MC);
d.
m. Nov. 30, 1923 Frank Romine Taylor, he was born
   Oct. 1, 1897 (MC).

   CHILDREN:

JACK CROSSMAN-11 TAYLOR, b. Nov. 9, 1924 (MC);
   m. Sept. 13, 1952 Elizabeth Miller, she was born
      May 1, 1924 (MC).
   Children:
      PAMELA JANE-12 TAYLOR, b. May 25, 1955 (MC).

      FRANK ROMINE-12 TAYLOR, b. June 19, 1962 (MC).

JEAN GROVE-11 TAYLOR, b. April 26, 1927 (MC);
   d.
   m. unmarried as of 1965 (MC).

THOMAS ROMINE-11 TAYLOR, b. July 22, 1933 (MC);
   d.
   m. Aug. 4, 1954 Dorothy Thompson, she was born Feb.
      14, 1935.
   Children:
      THOMAS GRANT-12 TAYLOR, b. Jan. 17, 1956 (MC).

      WILLIAM WESLEY-12 TAYLOR, b. June 18, 1957 (MC).

      SUSAN MARIE-12 TAYLOR, b. Sept. 27, 1958 (MC).

      CAROL CROSSMAN-12 TAYLOR, b. Oct. 17, 1960 (MC).

                ****

GEORGE ISAAC-10 CROSSMAN   (George-9, Isaac-8, Asa-7, Asa-6,
                            James-5, Joseph-4, Joseph-3,
                            Robert-2, John-1)

b. Dec. 5, 1900 (MC);
d.
m. May 15, 1925 Bessie M. Diefenbach, she was born Aug.
   20, 1903 (MC).

CHILDREN:

GEORGE ROBERT-11 CROSSMAN, b. June 25, 1926 (MC);
   d.
   m. Nov. 23, 1956 Rita Kay _____, she was born June
      30, 1933 (MC).

   Children:

      JAMES LEE-12 CROSSMAN, b. June 16, 1959 (MC);

      NANCY ANN-12 CROSSMAN, b. June 30, 1961 (MC).

      DIANA RUTH-12 CROSSMAN, b. July 5, 1963 (MC).

****

see page
517

DALE FOREST-10 CROASMUN (William-9, Nathan-8, Asa-7, Asa-6,
                         James-5, Joseph-4, Joseph-3,
                         Robert-2, John-1)

b. May 15, 1887 (MC);
d. Oct. 24, 1941 (MC);
m. Sept. 11, 1920 Seeley Juanity Porter, she was born on
   April 11, 1886 (MC).

   CHILDREN:

FLORENCE "Flo Betty" ELIZABETH-11 CROASMUN, b.July 12,1921(MC);
   m. July 12, 1962 Kenneth Frederick Brandon, b.Oct.17,1931(MC);
      they had no children (MC).
WILLIAM ARTHUR-11 CROASMUN, b. Oct. 5, 1922 (MC);
   m. Dec. 27, 1953 Ruth Louise DeWalt, b.Oct.7,1928(MC).
   Children:
      CLIFFORD NELSON-12 CROASMUN, b. Jan.30,1960 (MC).
      SUSAN MARIE-12 CROASMUN, b.   ; d. died at birth (MC).
      CONNIE LEE-12 CROASMUN, b. April 27, 1962 (MC).
DALE FOREST-11 CROASMUN, Jr., b.Nov.21,1927 (MC);
   m. Aug. 28, 1954 Sandra Ann McFarland, b.Dec.6,1932(MC).
   Children:
      LYNN ANN-12 CROASMUN, b. Feb. 26, 1956 (MC).
      STEVEN FOREST-12 CROASMUN, b. Sept. 26, 1957 (MC).
NATHAN PORTER-11 CROASMUN, b. March 11, 1929 (MC);
   m. Feb. 14, 1953 Glenyce Joette "Glenny Jo" Richards,
      she was born Feb. 11, 1932 (MC).
   Children:
      DALE ALBERT-12 CROASMUN, b. Jan. 3, 1954 (MC);
        m. Sept. 14, 1974 Joy Elizabeth Eck, she was born
           on Nov. 27, 1955 (MC).
      KATHRYN ANN-12 CROASMUN, b. Dec. 27, 1957 (MC);
        m. Oct. 23, 1977 Douglas Allen Hepler, he was born
           on July 19, 1957 (MC).
      JEANNE CELESTE-12 CROASMUN, b. Feb. 26, 1961 (MC).

      NATHAN PORTER-12 CROASMUN, b. Dec. 6, 1966 (MC).

****

see page
518

IRIS MARTHA-10 CROASMUN   (John-9, Nathan-8, Asa-7, Asa-6,
                          James-5, Joseph-4, Joseph-3,
                          Robert-2, John-1)
b. June 19, 1889 at St. Louis, MO   (MC);
d.
m. May 27, 1917 Forrest Fremont Calkins, he was born on
   April 11, 1889 and he died Feb. 21, 1951 (MC).

   CHILDREN:

JAMES EDWARD-11 CALKINS, b.Dec.13,1923 (MC);
   d.
   m. Feb. 14, 1948 Mollie Steinbacker, born Aug. 16,
      1922 (MC); they have no children (MC).

FORREST PARKER-11 CALKINS, b. June 21, 1921 (MC);
   d.
   m. Feb. 28, 1942 Ellen Longstreth, born Feb. 21, 1921(MC).
   Children:
      GREGORY ALAN-12 CALKINS, b. March 2, 1949 (MC).

      MICHAEL DOUGLAS-12 CALKINS, b. Jan. 18, 1951 (MC).

      ELLEN KATHLEEN-12 CALKINS, b. Oct. 10, 1955 (MC).

      RICHARD EUGENE-12 CALKINS, b. March 23, 1964 (MC).

****

Genealogy of the Crossman Family, Supplement #3 • ©1990 by Robert Owen Crossman • 908 Front • Conway, AR 72032

see page
518

EDITH RAY-10 CROASMUN   (John-9, Nathan-8, Asa-7, Asa-6,
                    James-5, Joseph-4, Joseph-3,
                    Robert-2, John-1)
b. Oct. 23, 1891 Alexandria, LA (MC);
d. May   1948 (MC);
m. John Eugene Frampton (MC).

CHILDREN:

JOHN EUGENE-11 FRAMPTON, b. June 19, 1916 (MC);
    m. April 19, 1941 Marim Anna Holman, born May 4,1914(MC).
    Children:
    JOHN GORDON-12 FRAMPTON, b. Jan. 31, 1942 (MC);
        d. March 6, 1959 (MC).

    MARY ELAINE-12 FRAMPTON, b. March 15, 1944 (MC).

    ANN KATHLEEN-12 FRAMPTON, b. Aug. 8, 1945 (MC).

    DOUGLAS STEWART-12 FRAMPTON, b. Dec. 8, 1946 (MC).

    DONALD PAUL-12 FRAMPTON, b. May 6, 1948 (MC).

    PETER JOSEPH-12 FRAMPTON, b. Feb. 10, 1951 (MC).

IRIS GERALDINE-11 FRAMPTON, b. Nov. 27, 1919 (MC);
    m. Aug. 6, 1944 William Mabry, born Sept. 16,1920 (MC).
    Children:

    MARY ANN-12 MABRY, b. March 4, 1946 (MC).

    JEANNETTE-12 MABRY, b. Nov. 4, 1954 (MC).

DOUGLAS STEWART-11 FRAMPTON, b. June 19, 1921 (MC);
    d. 1944 killed in action during Worl War II, in an
    airplane in South Pacific (MC).

****

see page
518

GERALDINE MAE-10 CROASMUN (John-9,Nathan-8,Asa-7,Asa-6,
James-5, Joseph-4, Joseph-3,
Robert-2, John-1)

b. May 3, 1894 (MC);
d.
m. Dec. 25, 1919 Gerald MacKenzie, he was born Jan. 22,
   1891 (MC).

   CHILDREN:

GERALD-11 MACKENZIE, b. Aug. 3, 1922 (MC);
  m. Nov. 24, 1944 June Raymond, she was born Nov. 24,1924(MC).
  Children:

    ALLISON CAROL-12 MACKENZIE, b. March 18, 18, 1949(MC).

    JANET VICTORIA-12 MACKENZIE, b. Aug. 7, 1951 (MC).

CAROL-11 MACKENZIE, b. Feb. 10, 1926 (MC);
  m. Sept. 9, 1950 Donald Gustoff, b.Dec. 14, 1926 (MC).
  Children:

    DAVID IAN-12 GUSTOFF, b. Sept. 30, 1952 (MC).

    WILLIAM KENT-12 GUSTOFF, b. Feb. 10, 1956 (MC);

    JOHNATHAN STEWART-12 GUSTOFF, b. Jan. 5, 1958 (MC).

****

see page
521

IRA DWIGHT-10 SEILER (Henrietta-9, Asa-8, Asa-7, Asa-6,
                James-5, Joseph-4, Joseph-3,
                Robert-2, John-1)
b. Oct. 16, 1877 (MC);
d. Aug. 9, 1957 (MC);
m.(1) Dec.   , 1903 Jessie Shepherd (MC);
m.(2)   Christine Swanson (MC);
m.(3)   Alda Warren (MC).

     CHILDREN:

MIRIAM-11 SEILER, b.   (MC).
   m. Neil Quartel, a doctor (MC).
   Children:
      JOANNE-12 QUARTEL, b.   (MC);
        m. Donald Watson (MC); divorced (MC).
        m.(2) John Monahan (MC).
        Children:
           DAVID-13 WATSON, b.   (MC).
      WILLIAM-12 QUARTEL, b.   (MC).
      DEBORAH-12 QUARTEL, b.   (MC).

MARVINE SHEPHERD-11 SEILER, b.   (MC);
   m. Ray Collins (MC);
   Children:

      RICHARD DWIGHT-12 COLLINS, b. 1937 (MC);
      JESSIE SUZANNE-12 COLLINS, b.   (MC);
        m. Paul Trentham (MC).
        Children:
           PAULA SUE-13 TRENTHAM, b.   (MC).
           RICHARD RAY-13 TRENTHAM, b. 1964 (MC).

             ****

THOMAS O.-10 ENTERLINE   (Mary-9, Asa-8, Asa-7, Asa-6,
                          James-5, Joseph-4, Joseph-3,
                          Robert-2, John-1)

    b. March 7, 1883 (MC);
    d. April 8, 1966 (MC);
    m. June 28, 1911 Zelda Rae Kuntz, she was born Jan.30,1889(MC).
       CHILDREN:

    MARIM ELIZABETH-11 ENTERLINE, b.March 22, 1913 (MC);
       m.May 6,1945 Donald Fred Manke, b.Dec.31,1912 (MC); they
          live at Oakmont, Pennsylvania (MC).
       Children:
          PAUL T.-12 MANKE, b. April 21, 1947 (MC).
          DONEL RUTH-12 MANKE, b. May 30,1948 (MC).
    ALLISON KUNTZ-11 ENTERLINE, b. June 26, 1914 (MC);
       m.Sept.26,1945 Dorcas Edwards, b. June 30, 1918 (MC);
          they live at Edgewood, Pennsylvania (MC).
       Children:
          MARY J.-12 ENTERLINE, b. May 17, 1948 (MC).
          LINDA C.-12 ENTERLINE, b. April 13, 1950 (MC).
    JOSEPHINE-11 ENTERLINE, b. Aug. 26, 1915 (MC);
       m.Aug. 8,1945 Charles Stanley Morris, b.April 13,1913(MC).
          they live at Oliveburg, Pennsylvania (MC).
       Children:
          CAROL LEE-12 MORRIS, b. Dec. 7, 1947 (MC).
          SUSAN E.-12 MORRIS, b. Dec. 21, 1950 (MC).
    THOMAS GAYLE-11 ENTERLINE, b.Jan.10,1917 (MC);
       m.Feb.4,1960 Nelle Jackish, b.Nov.4,1917 (MC); they live
          at White Oaks, Pennsylvania (MC).
    DONALD RAY-11 ENTERLINE, b.June 18,1918 (MC);
       m.Aug.22,1941 Ethel Ritter, b. July 29,1918 (MC); they
          live at Pittsburg, Pennsylvania (MC).
    AGNES MAXINE-11 ENTERLINE, b.Feb.17, 1922 (MC);
       m.Sept.2,1950 William Schaper, b.Nov.1,1923(MC); they
          live at Thorton, California (MC).
       Children:
          JEFFREY LYNN-12 SCHAPER, b.Sept.23,1952, twin (MC).
          JENNIFER LINN-12 SCHAPER, b.Sept.23,1952, twin (MC).
          JOHN LINN-12 SCHAPER, b.Jan.6,1954 (MC).
          JEANINE LINN-12 SCHAPER, b. Oct. 22, 1955 (MC).
    JOHN WILLIAM-11 ENTERLINE, b.May 8, 1924 (MC);
       m.Dec. 31, 1959 Alice Marie Bottenhorn, b.July 6,1927(MC).
       Children:
          WILLIAM THOMAS-12 ENTERLINE, b.June 4,1961 (MC).
          NANCY JO-12 ENTERLINE, b. Aug. 13, 1962 (MC).
          ROBERT J.-12 ENTERLINE, b. Feb. 22, 1964 (MC).

****

see page
525

EFFA BEULAH-10 CROASMUN   (Everett-9,Asa-8,Asa-7,Asa-6,
                          James-5, Joseph-4, Joseph-3,
                          Robert-2, John-1)
b. Feb. 17, 1888 (MC);
d. July 7, 1963 (MC);
m. Dec. 25, 1915 Harry Leroy Ramsley (MC).

    CHILDREN:

TWILA MARY-11 RAMSLEY, b.Sept. 8, 1916 (MC);
    m. Leroy Steel (MC).
    Children:
        BETTY JO-12 STEEL, b.   (MC).
        MYRA ALICE-12 STEEL, b.   (MC).

HARRY THOMAS-11 RAMSLEY, b.March 5, 1918 (MC);
    m. Virginia Wolff (MC).

HELEN MAY-11 RAMSLEY, b. May 14, 1919 (MC);
    m. William Bowser (MC).
    Children:

        TWILA MARGARET-12 BOWSER, b.   (MC).

        CHARLOTTE DARLENE-12 BOWSER, b.   (MC).

        JANET MARIE-12 BOWSER, b.   (MC).

DOROTHY JANE-11 RAMSLEY, b. April 28, 1920 (MC);
    m. Lloyd Barnett (MC).
    Children:

        DONALD-12 BARNETT, b.   (MC).

                    ****

PAUL STEVENS-10 CROSSMAN   (Everett-9, Asa-8, Asa-7, Asa-6, James-5,
                            Joseph-4, Joseph-3, Robert-2, John-1)
b. Dec. 18, 1890 (MC);
d.
m. June 15, 1918 Margaret Seitz, she was born Dec. 3, 1889 (MC).
Paul Stevens Croasmun changed spelling of name to "Crossman" (DC).

CHILDREN (of Paul & Margaret):
  MARYBELLE-11 CROSSMAN, b. Dec. 28, 1919 Meadville, PA (MC);
    m. Dec. 6, 1942 Henry Mendenhall Taylor Haris, b. Nov. 26, 1918(MC).
    Children:
        MARY ANN-12 HARRIS, b. Dec. 4, 1943 (MC);
          m. July 25, 1970 Charles Russell Dunn, b. April 7, 1944 (MC).
          Children:
              LINDSAY ANN-13 DUNN, b. Nov. 11, 1974 (MC).
        HENRY TAYLOR-12 HARRIS, b. April9, 1947 (MC);
          m. Aug. 17, 1968 Patricia Jean Bushell, b. Oct. 1, 1946 (MC)..
          Children:
              SHAWN-13 HARRIS, b. May 19, 1972 (MC).
              ASHLEY DALE-13 HARRIS, b. Dec. 31, 1974 (MC).
        ROBERT -12 HARRIS, b. March 20, 1957 (MC).
        NANCY LEE-12 HARRIS, b. June 16, 1959 (MC).
  PAULINE-11 CROSSMAN, b. June 8, 1921 at Sea Cliff, N.J. (MC).
    m. Aug. 19, 1943 Warren Charles Kilkebeck, b. Nov. 22, 1920 (MC).
    Children:
        WARREN CHARLES-12 KOLKEBECK, Jr. b. Sept. 8, 1945 (MC).
          m. Oct. 12, 1968 Lorienne Mary Fey, b. March 5, 1946 (MC).
        JOANNE-12 KILKEBECK, b. Feb. 23, 1949 (MC);
          m. Jed Laputka (MC).
          Children:
              POLLY-12 LAPUTKA, b. May 9, 1977 (MC);
                d. Aug. __, 1977 "infant crib death" (MC).
  JANET LOUISE-11 CROSSMAN, b. April 21, 1925 Girard, PA (MC);
    m(1) May 16, 1947 Charles E. Miller, b. Feb. 5, 1927 (MC);
    m(2) Wilber Davis, b. March ___, 192_.
    Children (of Janet and Charles):
        MARGARET ROSE-12 MILLER, b. May 5, 1948 (MC).
        CHARLES E.P.-12 MILLER, b. July 20, 1950 (MC).
        MITCHELL ALLEN-12 MILLER, b. Jan. 16, 1952 (MC).
        THOMAS PAUL-12 MILLER, b. March 21, 1954 (MC).
        KIRK SEITZ-12 MILLER, b. July 26, 1959 (MC).
  PAUL SEITZ-11 CROSSMAN, b. April 18, 1927 Girard, PA (MC);
    m. Jan. 2, 1954 Janet Elaine Munson, b. May 26, 1931 (MC);
    Children (of Paul and Janet)
        APRIL ANN-12 CROSSMAN, b. April 26, 1955 (MC).
        JILL ELAINE-12 CROSSMAN, b. June 12, 1957 (MC)
        LYNN LOUISE-12 CROSSMAN, b. Sept. 23, 1960 (MC).

Genealogy of the Crossman Family, Supplement #3 • ©1990 by Robert Owen Crossman • 901 Front Street • Conway, Arkansas 72032

NANNIE LULA-10 CROASMUN (Everett-9,Asa-8,Asa-7,Asa-6,
                        James-5, Joseph-4, Joseph-3,
                        Robert-2, John-1)
  b. Jan. 2, 1893 (MC);
  d. Aug. 19, 1963 (MC);
  m. April 12, 1916 J. Boyd Smith, he was born Sept. 28,1894
     and he died Jan. 13, 1978 (MC).

     CHILDREN:

RUTH-11 SMITH, b.Jan.12,1917 Erie, PA (MC);
   m. Harold St.John(MC).
   Children:
      TERRY-12 ST.JOHN., b.Feb.17,1941 (MC);
         m. Mary Jane Boritz (MC).
         Children:
            SUZHANNA-13 ST.JOHN, b.   (MC).
            TODD-13 ST.JOHN, b.   (MC).
      ROBERT-12 ST.JOHN, b. Aug. 12, 1942 (MC);
         m. Sandra Elizabeth Bastian (MC).
         Children:
            SCOTT-13 ST.JOHN, b.   (MC).
            CINDA LEE-13 ST.JOHN, b.   (MC).
      MICHAEL-12 ST.JOHN, b. June 1, 1944 (MC);
         m. Jane M. Russell (MC).
         Children:
            SHANNON KAY-13 ST.JOHN, b.   (MC).
            CHILD-13 ST.JOHN, b.   (MC).
      THOMAS-12 ST.JOHN, b. Oct. 26, 1946 (MC).
see page
593 MARIE-11 SMITH, b. Nov.11,1918 Puxsutanny,PA (MC);
       m.March 20,1939 Leslie Murray, b. June 30,1918 (MC).

PAUL RICHARD-11 SMITH, b.Nov.23,1919 (MC);d.Feb.10,1964(MC);
   m.July 16,1944 Margarita Kaberlein, b.Oct.5,1920(MC).
   Children:
      DWIGHT BOYD-12 SMITH,b.Aug.20,1946;m.June 7,1969 Rita Black,
         she was born Sept. 20,1946 (MC).

                  ****

Information on this page supplied by Marion Croasmun of
Valier, PA in 1978.

Genealogy of the Crossman Family, Supplement #3 • ©1990 by Robert Owen Crossman • 908 Front • Conway, AR 72032

TWILA BELLE-10 CROASMUN   (Everett-9,Asa-8,Asa-7,Asa-6,
                            James-5, Joseph-4, Joseph-3,
  b. April 26,1895 (MC);   Robert-2, John-1)
  d. Aug. 10, 1977 (MC);
  m. James Carl Neal, he was born May 31, 1897, they were
     married on Sept. 28, 1918 (MC).

     CHILDREN:

MARY VIRGINIA-11 NEAL, b. April 19, 1920 (MC);
   m. April 15,1950 Joseph James Sorce, b.Oct.26,1926(MC).
   Children: (live at 316 Crescent Dr., Erie, PA)
      CHARLES CARLTON-12 SORCE, b. Feb. 28, 1951 (MC).
      CHRISTOPHER NEAL-12 SORCE, b. Oct. 16,1952 (MC).
      GREGORY JOSEPH-12 SORCE, b. May 23, 1955. (MC).
KATHRYN IRENE-11 NEAL, b. May 7, 1924 (MC);
   m.Dec. 13,1947 Charles D. Bugher born May 24,1921(MC);
   they live in Monaca, PA (MC).
   Children:
      MARY ANN-12 BUGHER, b.July 28,1949 (MC);
        m(1) Aug.1,1970 John William Ide (MC);
        m(2) Oct. 19,1974 Fred Schroyer born Dec.27,1943(MC).
        Children:
           LAURA MARIE-13 SCHROYER, b.Aug.11, 1975 (MC).
           KRESTINA DIANE-13 SCHROYER, b.Feb.19,1977 (MC).
      CAROL IRENE-12 BUGHER, b.Dec.12,1950 (MC);
        m. Nov.18,1970 Walter Ward, born Sept.28,1950 (MC).
        Children: (lived in Anchorage, Alaska in 1977)
           MARY LOU-13 WARD, b. Dec. 13, 1974 (MC).
           MATTHEW BENJAMIN-13 WARD, b. June 11, 1977 (MC).
      WARD CHARLES-12 BUGHER, b. May 28, 1957 (MC).
PHYLLIS-11 NEAL, b. July 25, 1935 (MC);
   m. Nov.2,1968 Arthur M. Cooper, born Jan.13,1941 (MC);
   they live at Orchard Park, N.Y. in 1978 (MC).
   Children:
      BENJAMIN JOSEPH-12 COOPER, b. March 21, 1971 (MC).

                ****

All material on this page supplied by Marion Croasmun of
Valier, PA in 1978.

Genealogy of the Crossman Family, Supplement #3 • ©1990 by Robert Owen Crossman • 908 Front • Conway, AR 72032

see page
526

NAOMI-10 CROASMUN (Isaac-9, Asa-8, Asa-7, Asa-6,
                              James-5, Joseph-4, Joseph-3,
    b. April 27, 1894 (MC); Robert-2, John-1)
    d.
    m. Nov. 24, 1915 John C. Emhoff, he was born Dec.11,1896(MC).

        CHILDREN:

see page
594
DONNA BELLE-11 EMHOFF, b. June 10,1916 (MC);
        m.July 4, 1942 Clarence Eugene Postwaite (MC).

see page
595
ELLA MAE-11 EMHOFF, b. May 23, 1917 (MC);
        m(1) Ernie Helm (MC);
        m(2) March 23,1939 John Pemberthy, born Sept.28,1916(MC).

see page
596
EILEEN-11 EMHOFF, b. Sept. 14, 1918 (MC);
        m. George Whitfield (MC).

DRUCILLA-11 EMHOFF, b. Jan. 5, 1920 (MC);
        m. Nov. 5, 1955 Kenneth Allen, born May 18, 1922 (MC).

see page
597
WANDA-11 EMHOFF, b. April 24, 1921 (MC);
        m. Milford Evans, they divorced (MC);
        m(2) Aug.15,1972 Paul Jordon (MC).

see page
598
JOHN "Jack"-11 EMHOFF, b. Nov. 2, 1922 (MC);
        m. Nov. 28, 1942 Martha Benson, born July 24,1919(MC).

ELVIN-11 EMHOFF, b. Feb. 26, 1924 (MC);
    m. Elva A. Barnett (MC).
    Children:
      REGINA-12 EMHOFF, b. 1948 (MC).
      GARY-12 EMHOFF, b. 1949 (MC).
      THOMAS-12 EMHOFF, b. 1959 (MC).
      JOHN-12 EMHOFF, b.   (MC).

JOSEPH-11 EMHOFF, b. Nov. 1, 1925 (MC);
    m. 1960 Rita Halfeldt (MC).
    Children:
      MARK-12 EMHOFF, b. 1960 (MC).
      KURT-12 EMHOFF, b.   (MC).

****

Information on this page was supplied by Marion Croasmun of
Valier, PA in 1978.

Genealogy of the Crossman Family, Supplement #3 • ©1990 by Robert Owen Crossman • 908 Front • Conway, AR 72032

MABEL FLORENCE-10 OBERLIN (Augusta-9, Asa-8, Asa-7, Asa-6,
                     James-5, Joseph-4, Joseph-3,
                     Robert-2, John-1)
b. Nov. 30, 1884 (MC);
d. May 4, 1970 (MC);
m.   1901 Lester E. Faulk, he died in 1966 (MC).

     CHILDREN:

HELEN-11 FAULK, b. 1902 (MC);
   d. Oct. 4, 1964 (MC);
   m. Richard A. Lacy (MC).
      Children:

        RICHARD ALBERT-12 LACY III, b. 1929 (MC).
          m. Anita Holman(MC); live in Greensboro, N.C.(MC).

            Children:

              MARGARET-13 LACY, b. 1956 (MC).

              CHARLES OBERLIN-13 LACY, b. 1961 (MC).

        ANN-12 LACY, b.   (MC).
          Ann lives in Bristol, Virginia (MC).

CATHERINE-11 FAULK, b.   1907 (MC);
   m. DeWitt Tucker (MC); no children (MC).

****

see page
528

SUE MAURINE-10 STEVENS   (Susan-9, Asa-8, Asa-7, Asa-6,
                    James-5, Joseph-4, Joseph-3,
                    Robert-2, John-1)
b.   1901 (MC);
d.
m.   1928 Richard Howard Morrison, he was born
    in 1896 and he died in 1939 (MC).

    CHILDREN:

MARY SUE-11 MORRISON, b.   1930 (MC);
    m.(1)   1949 Walter Gardner, he was born July
        15, 1927 (MC);
    m.(2)   1965 Gene Ahlf (MC).
    Children: (all by first marriage)
        GARY-12 GARDNER, b.   1950 (MC).

        GAIL-12 GARDNER, b.   1951 (MC).

MAURINE-11 MORRISON, b.   1932 (MC);
    m. 1951 Preston Bixby Hatchkiss, he was born 1929 (MC).
    Children:
        HILARY-12 HATCHKISS, b.   1957 (MC).

        BIXBY-12 HATCHKISS, b. April   1963 (MC).

        BRIAN-12 HATCHKISS, b. April   1966 (MC).

RICHARD HOWARD-11 MORRISON II, b.   1936 (MC);
    m. 1966 Laura Cockburn (MC).
    Children:
        RICHARD HOWARD-12 MORRISON III, b.   1967 (MC).

        PETER-12 MORRISON, b.   1967 (MC).

****

ELIZABETH BLANCHE-10 DORMIRE   (Mary-9, Miles-8, Asa-7, Asa-6,
James-5, Joseph-4, Joseph-3,
Robert-2, John-1)

b. June 21, 1903 (MC);
d.
m. April 29, 1939 John Quincey Hoover, he was born Dec.
23, 1901 (MC).

CHILDREN:

MARY ANN-11 HOOVER, b. Sept. 23, 1940 (MC);
   m.Nov.2,1963 Charles Neal Miller, born Aug. 5,1941(MC).
   Children:
      NANCY ELIZABETH-12 MILLER, b. Nov. 15, 1966 (MC).
      NEALA ANN-12 MILLER, b. Oct. 4, 1969 (MC).
JOHN CURTIS-11 HOOVER, b. March 11, 1942 (MC);
   m. June 21, 1963 Donna Mae Custer, born May 5,1939(MC).
   Children:
      JOHN WESLEY-12 HOOVER, b. Jan. 19, 1969 (MC).
      DANIEL CURTIS-12 HOOVER, b. Nov. 4, 1973, twin (MC).
      SAMUEL LEE-12 HOOVER, b. Nov. 5, 1973, twin (MC);
         they are twin but because of midnight births, they
         are recorded on different days (MC).
ELLA MAE-11 HOOVER, b. March 6, 1943 (MC);
   m. Aug. 27, 1966 Larry Marshall (MC).
   Children:
      DAVID ALLEN-12 MARSHALL, b. Feb. 9, 1967 (MC).
      PAMELA ANN-12 MARSHALL, b. June 30, 1970 (MC).
DAVID LEE-11 HOOVER, b. April 27, 1947 (MC);
   m. May 16, 1970 Wanda Wells (MC).
   Children:
      LEONARD LEROY-12 HOOVER, b. Dec. 27, 1970 (MC).
      JAY WAYNE-12 HOOVER, b. May 10, 1975 (MC).

****

MARY ELVIRA-10 DORMIRE   (Mary-9, Miles-8, Asa-7, Asa-6,
                    James-5, Joseph-4, Joseph-3,
                    Robert-2, John-1)
b. Aug. 30, 1909 (MC);
d.
m. June 1, 1933 Robert Irvin Heitzenrater, he was born
    Aug. 1, 1908 (MC).

    CHILDREN:

ROBERT IRVIN-11 HEITZENRATER, b. Dec. 6, 1933 (MC);
  m. June 22, 1957 Sally Lou Sprankle, born Dec.15,1934(MC).
  Children:
    DWIGHT TAYLOR-12 HEITZENRATER, b. May 12, 1960 (MC).
    TROY LELAND-12 HEITZENRATER, b. Feb. 8, 1963 (MC).
MARGARET EMILY "Peg"-11 HEITZENRATER, b.Sept.5,1935(MC);
  m.April 30,1961 William Edward Harris, born Oct.6,1938(MC).
  Children:
    DIANNA LYNN-12 HARRIS, b. Jan. 10, 1969 (MC).
    JILL DENISE-12 HARRIS, b. Feb. 16, 1971 (MC).
WILLIAM HOWARD-11 HEITZENRATER, b. Feb. 20, 1944 (MC);
  d. June 10,1971 in a tractor accident (MC).
JON RANDALL-11 HEITZENRATER, b. May 11,1945 (MC);
  m. Aug.26,1967 Lois Andrea Kimble, born June 19,1945(MC).
  Children:
    CLARK DAVID-12 HEITZENRATER, b.March 17, 1969 (MC).
    WILLIAM HOWARD-12 HEITZENRATER, b. Feb. 18, 1972 (MC).
GREGORY THOMAS-11 HEITZENRATER, b. May 21, 1948 (MC);
  m.   1965 Janet Thomas, born May 9, 1948 (MC).
  Children:
    DOUGLAS GREGORY-12 HEITZENRATER, b.June 30,1966 (MC).
    BRYAN MATTHEW-12 HEITZENRATER, b. June 30, 1968 (MC).

****

Genealogy of the Crossman Family, Supplement #3 • ©1990 by Robert Owen Crossman • 908 Front • Conway, AR 72032

MILDRED JANE-10 CROASMUN, (William-9, Miles-8, Asa-7, Asa-6,
                    James-5, Joseph-4, Joseph-3,
                    Robert-2, John-1)
b. Aug. 3, 1907 (MC);
d.
m.   James Monroe Whitaker, he was born on Feb.
   6, 1900 (MC).
   CHILDREN:

GLEN CROASMUN-11 WHITAKER, b. April 30,1928 Kona,KY (MC);
   d.
   m.   Mary Hall (MC).
   Children:
      DEBRA-12 WHITAKER, b.   (MC).
      GLEN CROASMUN-12 WHITAKER, b.   (MC).
      DONNA-12 WHITAKER, b.   (MC).

CLARA SUE-11 WHITAKER, b. Dec. 2, 1932 Payne Gap, KY (MC);
   d.
   m.   Rodney Sexton (MC).
   Children:
      RODNEY-12 SEXTON, Jr., b.   (MC);
       d. "died" (MC).
      JAMES-12 SEXTON, b.   (MC).

****

see page
530

HELEN OLIVE-10 CROASMUN   (William-9, Miles-8, Asa-7, Asa-6,
                    James-5, Joseph-4, Joseph-3,
                    Robert-2, John-1)
b. Feb. 10, 1912 (MC);
d.
m. Dec. 16, 1931 Paul N. Lusk, he was born Jan. 10, 1909(MC).

    CHILDREN:

THALIA VALJEAN-11 LUSK, b. Sept. 15, 1933 (MC);
    m.   Melvin Childers (MC).
    Children:
       HELEN-12 CHILDERS, b.   (MC).
       MELVIN-12 CHILDERS, b.   (MC).
JEROME-11 LUSK, b. Aug. 23, 1936 (MC).

CLIFTON-11 LUSK, b. July 11, 1939 (MC).

JANICE-11 LUSK, b. Feb. 1, 1943 (MC).

KAREN ANN-11 LUSK, b. July 3, 1946 (MC).

CATHY EIIEEN-11 LUSK, b. May 24, 1950 (MC).

****

see page
531

NELLIE JANE-10 CROASMUN   (Nathan-9, Miles-8, Asa-7, Asa-6.
                           James-5, Joseph-4, Joseph-3,
                           Robert-2, John-1)

b. Sept. 16, 1911 (MC);
d.
m. Sept. 19, 1928 Wilbur Leroy Sheesley, he was born on
   March 23, 1907 (MC).

   CHILDREN:

JOHN LEONARD-11 SHEESLEY, b.Sept.29,1929 (MC);
   d.March 29, 1932 (MC); died in childhood (MC).
EVELYN LUCILLE-11 SHEESLEY, b. Feb.5,1931 (MC);
   m. Jan. 3,1949 Robert James Snyder, born Jan.3,1926(MC).
   Children:
      NANCY LEE-12 SNYDER, b. May 22, 1949 (MC).
      BOYD ALLEN-12 SNYDER, b. Dec. 14, 1950 (MC).
      LINDA JANE-12 SNYDER, b. Dec. 28, 1951 (MC).
      JAMES DELO-12 SNYDER, b. July 12, 1953 (MC).
      ROBERT JAMES-12 SNYDER, b. July 14, 1961 (MC).
      JANET IRENE-12 SNYDER, b. Nov. 13, 1963 (MC).
CHARLES RAY-11 SHEESLEY, b.Jan. 5, 1933 (MC);
   m.Sept.8,1956 Eva Myrtle Lloyd, born Oct.21, 1931(MC).
   Children:
      JOY LYNN-12 SHEESLEY, b.March 31,1957 (MC).
      VALERIE ANN-12 SHEESLEY, b. June 16, 1958 (MC).
      PAMELA SUE-12 SHEESLEY, b. Nov. 21, 1960 (MC).
      CHARLES RAY-12 SHEESLEY, b. Nov. 13, 1963 (MC).
ROBERT BURTON-11 SHEESLEY, b.Dec.21,1934 (MC);
   m.June 4,1954 Doris Vasbinder, born May 29,1936 (MC).
   Children:
      ROBERTA ALLEN-12 SHEESLEY, b.March 24,1959 (MC).
      ROBERT MARTIN-12 SHEESLEY, b.May 4,1960 (MC).
      KENNETH LEROY-12 SHEESLEY, b.May 20,1962 (MC).
BYRON MURTON-11 SHEESLEY, b.Feb.3,1936 (MC);
   m.April 21,1962 Earlene Gilbert, born Feb.18,1940(MC).
   Children:
      DOUGLAS TROY-12 SHEESLEY, b.Jan. 1,1963 (MC).
JOYCE ANN-11 SHEESLEY, b.Dec.4,1937 (MC);
   m.May 30,1959 Donald Eugene Kerr, born Nov.5,1937(MC).
   Children:
      SALLY DETTE-12 KERR, b. Oct. 7, 1961 (MC).
      WILLIAM BOYD-12 KERR, b.May 7,1963 (MC).
BARBARA LEE-11 SHEESLEY, b.Feb.23,1944 (MC);
   b.Feb.22,1964 Lloyd Fisher, born Nov.11,1939 (MC).
   Children:
      MELISSA SUE-12 FISHER, b.Sept.2,1964 (MC).
      LESLIE-12 FISHER, b. Jan. 10, 1969 (MC).
      ERNEST LEROY-12 FISHER, b. July 8, 1970 (MC).

****

LULA ALICE-10 CROASMUN (Daniel-9, James-8, Asa-7, Asa-6,
              James-5, Joseph-4, Joseph-3,
              Robert-2, John-1)
b. Dec. 16, 1887 (MC);
d. July 26, 1967 (MC);
m. Feb. 10, 1908 Saul Johnson, he was born on April 2,
   1886 and he died in 1975 (MC).

CHILDREN:

MARY EVELYN-11 JOHNSON, b. Nov. 13, 1908 (MC);
   d. June 20, 1963 (MC);
   m. Nov. 24, 1945 Bert Gamble (MC).

RUTH GERALDINE-11 JOHNSON, b. Nov. 9, 1911 (MC);
   d.
   m. Oct.28,1937 Carl P. Dingledy II (MC).
   Children:
      CARL PHILIP-12 DINGLEDY , b. June 7, 1943 (MC);
         m. Oct. 2,1965 Frances Marie Pussateri, she was
            born Sept. 5, 1945 (MC).

      JAY RANDALL-12 DINGLEDY, b.June 28, 1947 (MC);
         m. June 14, 1969 Carol Chisholm (MC).
         Children:

            LINDSAY MARGARET-13 DINGLEDY, b.Nov.18,1976(MC).

RUSSELL LEROY-11 JOHNSON, b. May 2, 1914 (MC);
   d.
   m. Sept. 29, 1956 Cordelia P. Sollers (MC).
   Children:
      RUSSELL LEROY-12 JOHNSON, Jr., b. Aug. 5,1957 (MC).

      RONALD ERIE-12 JOHNSON, b. Feb. 6, 1960 (MC).

      RANDALL KEVIN-12 JOHNSON, b. Oct. 31, 1963 (MC).

MARGARET ANNABEL-11 JOHNSON, b. Oct. 4, 1916 (MC);
   d. Nov. 6, 1971 (MC);
   m. Feb. 10, 1949 Joseph J. Hudak (MC).

****

HOMER BURR-10 CROASMUN (Daniel-9, James-8, Asa-7. Asa-6.
                    James-5, Joseph-4, Joseph-3,
                    Robert-2, John-1)
   b. Jan. 31, 1890 (MC);
   d. Jan. 31, 1976 (MC);
   m. April 21, 1917 Alma Johnson, she was born Feb.28,1892(MC).

   CHILDREN:

DOROTHY VIRGINIA-11 CROASMUN, b. July 21, 1919 (MC);
   m. May 15, 1943 Robert Kelling (MC).
   Children:

      ROBERT LAWRENCE-12 KELLING, b. May 24, 1946 (MC);
         m. July 7, 1972 Sandra Corbett Mose (MC).
         Children: (step children)

            CHRISTINE LYNN-13 MOSS, b. 1965 (MC).

            MICHAEL STEFAN-13 MOSS, b. 1971 (MC).

      RICAHRD FLINT-12 KELLING, b. May 4, 1949 (MC);
         m. March 2, 1970 Carolyn Sue Dunn (MC).
         Children:

            RICHARD LAWRENCE-13 KELLING, b.Sept. 4, 1970 (MC).

      BETH NOELLE-12 KELLING, b. Jan. 6, 1954 (MC).

                  ****

573

SIDNEY-10 CROASMUN (Daniel-9, James-8, Asa-7, Asa-6,
                          James-5, Joseph-4, Joseph-3,
b. Jan. 17, 1894 (MC);   Robert-2, John-1)
d.
m. Oct. 16, 1915 Inez Smathers, she was born March 8,
   1892 (MC).

   CHILDREN:

ROBERT LEON-11 CROASMUN, b. July 13, 1919 (MC);
   d.
   m. Sept. 21, 1946 Beatrice Ruth Johnson (MC).
   Children:

      WILLIAM ROBERT-12 CROASMUN, b. June 7, 1953 (MC).

      JAMES DANIEL-12 CROASMUN, b. Jan. 31, 1955 (MC).

MARJORIE RUTH-11 CROASMUN, b. June 6, 1924 (MC);
   d.
   m. Sept. 13, 1947 Merle David Rester (MC).
   Children:

      THOMAS ALAN-12 RESTER, b. Sept. 2, 1948 (MC).

      LORI ANN-12 RESTER, b. Sept. 16, 1955 (MC).

****

Genealogy of the Crossman Family, Supplement #3 • ©1990 by Robert Owen Crossman • 908 Front • Conway, AR 72032

GERALDINE MARSH-10 CROASMUN (Daniel-9, James-8, Asa-7, Asa-6,
                    James-5, Joseph-4, Joseph-3,
                    Robert-2, John-1)
b. March 30, 1904 (MC);
d.
m. Aug. 23, 1923 George Plowman, he was born on June 21,
   1902 (MC).
   CHILDREN:

BETTY RUTH-11 PLOWMAN, b. May 23, 1924 (MC);
   m. Jan. 29, 1949 George Nunamaker (MC).
   Children:

      RICHARD ALLAN-12 NUNAMAKER, b. Aug. 4, 1951 (MC).

      HEIDI JEAN-12 NUNAMAKER, b. Jan. 26, 1954 (MC).

FLORENCE ARLENE-11 PLOWMAN, b. May 17, 1926 (MC);
   d. Aug. 30, 1928 (MC) died at age 2 years (MC).

MARGARET DARLENE-11 PLOWMAN, b.Jan. 29, 1934 (MC);
   m. July 2, 1960 Robert Eugene Nischivitz (MC).
   Children:

      ROBERT EUGENE-12 NISCHIVITZ, Jr., b. March 11, 1965(MC).

****

see page
532

ROBERT FRANK-10 CROASMUN (Daniel-9, James-8, Asa-7, Asa-6,
                James-5, Joseph-4, Joseph-3,
                Robert-2, John-1)
b. Oct. 1, 1906 (MC);
d.
m(1). Jan.   1932 Dorothy Famous, they divorced (MC);
m(2). Aug. 17, 1933 Gertrude McHoffie, she was born on
     July 28, 1907 (MC).

     CHILDREN:

ROBERTA MAE-11 CROASMUN, b. May 9, 1934 (MC);
  m. 1962 P. Alvin Larimer (MC).
  Children:

    MARY KATHRYN-12 LARIMER, b.   (MC).

    MARK KEVIN-12 LARIMER, b.   (MC).

    DOUGLAS ALLAN-12 LARIMER, b.   (MC).

ROBERT FRANK-11 CROASMUN, Jr., b. Feb. 3, 1940 (MC);
  m. Sept. 25, 1965 Karen Jean Riggs (MC).
  Children:

    JEFFREY RIGGS-12 CROASMUN, b. Oct. 9, 1967 (MC).

    KAREN JILL-12 CROASMUN, b. April 7, 1969 (MC).

JUDITH LOUISE-11 CROASMUN, b. Oct. 13, 1942 (MC);
  m. May 28, 1966 Robert Raines Lentz (MC).
  Children:

    SCOTT-12 LENTZ, b. Jan. 13, 1968 (MC).

    BRIAN CHRISTOPHER-12 LENTZ, b. May 9, 1970 (MC).

****

Genealogy of the Crossman Family, Supplement #3 • ©1990 by Robert Owen Crossman • 908 Front • Conway, AR 72032

MARGARET ISABEL-10 CROASMUN (Daniel-9, James-8, Asa-7, Asa-6,
James-5, Joseph-4, Joseph-3,
Robert-2, John-1)

b. Nov. 9, 1908 (MC);
d.
m. Sept. 27,1927 Charles Otto Neal, he was born on Nov.
27, 1901 and he died on Oct. 16, 1963 (MC).

CHILDREN:

MARGARET ARLENE-11 NEAL, b. March 29, 1929 (MC);
    m. Ted Potts, they are now divorced (MC).
    Children:
        MICHAEL-12 POTTS, b. May 21, 1953 (MC).
        JEFFREY NEAL-12 POTTS, b. May 6, 1958 (MC).
NANCY ANN-11 NEAL, b. July 14, 1934 (MC);
    m. Albert Meanor (MC).
    Children:
        COLIN-12 MEANOR, b. Oct. 6, 1957 (MC).
        KEVIN-12 MEANOR, b. Sept. 5, 1958 (MC).
        CHRIS-12 MEANOR, b. April 24, 1960 (MC).
        JON ROBERT-12 MEANOR, b. May 6, 1966, twin (MC).
        JENNIFER ANN-12 MEANOR, b. May 6, 1966 , twin (MC).
BONNIE JEAN-11 NEAL, b. March 22, 1939 (MC);
    m. William Stuchell (MC).
    Children:
        DENNIS-12 STUCHELL, b. July 22, 1959 (MC).
        DRENDA-12 STUCHELL, b. Nov. 1, 1962 (MC).
        JONATHAN NEAL-12 STUCHELL, b. May 26, 1966 (MC).
SUE ELAINE-11 NEAL, b. Jan. 29, 1946 (MC);
    m. David Gould (MC).
    Children:
        GREGORY-12 GOULD, b. May 27, 1964 (MC).
        PATRICK NEAL-12 GOULD, b. Dec. 22, 1967 (MC).
        JASON DAVID-12 GOULD, b. Oct. 2, 1970 (MC).

****

see page
532

DONALD HENRY "Pete"-10 CROASMUN   (Daniel-9, James-8, Asa-7,
                        Asa-6, James-5, Joseph-4, Joseph-3,
                        Robert-2, John-1)

b. May 16, 1912 (MC);
d. Nov. 25, 1977 (MC);
m. June 15, 1932 Katheryn Jane Kuntz, she was born Feb.
   11, 1915 (MC).

CHILDREN:

DONNA JAYNA-11 CROASMUN, b. Jan. 12, 1933 (MC);
   m. Sept. 15, 1956 William Dravesky, b. April 28,1931(MC).
   Children:
       CHEYRE LYNN-12 DRAVESKY, b. Aug. 2, 1957 (MC).
       DANIEL WILLIAM-12 DRAVESKY, b. April 27, 1959 (MC).
       JAYNE ANN-12 DRAVESKY, b. May 23, 1962 (MC).
       JOSEPH ANDREW-12 DRAVESKY, b. April 23, 1962 (MC).
       DEBRAH JEAN-12 DRAVESKY, b. Oct. 1, 1965 (MC).
DENNIS LEE-11 CROASMUN, b. Oct. 4, 1934 (MC);
   m. July 3, 1957 Doris Kloss, b. Nov. 27, 1940 (MC).
   Children:
       DONALD LEE-12 CROASMUN, b. July 10, 1958 (MC).
       DENNIS BARRY-12 CROASMUN, b. May 24, 1960 (MC).
       DARYL TODD-12 CROASMUN, b. June 6, 1961 (MC).
       DAVID ALLAN-12 CROASMUN, b. Aug. 13, 1963 (MC).
THOMAS JAY-11 CROASMUN, b. Nov. 6, 1936 (MC);
   m. June 15, 1958 Martha Jean Albanito, b.May 11,1937(MC).
   Children:
       MICHELLE-12 CROASMUN, b. Nov. 8, 1959 (MC).
       MICHAEL-12 CROASMUN, b. June 8, 1963 (MC).
       JEFFREY-12 CROASMUN, b. June 28, 1965 (MC).
DAVID HENRY-11 CROASMUN, b. July 31, 1938 (MC);
   m. March 21, 1959 Nancy Means, b. June 6, 1942 (MC).
   Children:
       LORI LYNN-12 CROASMUN, b. Sept. 10, 1959 (MC).
       DANIEL PATRICK-12 CROASMUN, b. March 23, 1962 (MC).
       JUDITH GAY-12 CROASMUN, b. June 19, 1966 (MC).
       MARK ALAN-12 CROASMUN, b. June 30, 1968 (MC).

****

Genealogy of the Crossman Family, Supplement #3 • ©1990 by Robert Owen Crossman • 908 Front • Conway, AR 72032

MARTHA ELIZABETH-10 DORMIRE (Ziela-9, Elizabeth-8, Asa-7, Asa-6, James-5, Joseph-4, Joseph-3, Robert-2, John-1)

b. May 9, 1910 (MC);
d.
m. July 8, 1933 Herbert Ross Wees , he was born April 23, 1901 and died March 9, 1966 (MC).

CHILDREN:

HERBERT ROSS-11 WEES , b. Aug. 26, 1934 (MC);
   d. March 7, 1969 (MC);
   m. June 22, 1960 Bonnie Meadows, b.May 6, 1939 (MC).
   Children:
      RICHARD ROSS-12 WEES, b. Oct. 18, 1962 (MC).
      KRISTEN ANN-12 WEES, b. Aug. 4, 1968 (MC).
JAMES ROBERT-11 WEES, b. May 17, 1936 (MC);
   m. Aug. 31, 1959 Patricia Scully, b. Oct.25,1939(MC).
   Children:
      MARTHA MARIE-12 WEES, b. Sept. 5, 1958 (MC).
      ELIZABETH ANN-12 WEES, b. Sept. 22, 1961 (MC).
MARVIN ANDREW-11 WEES, b. Jan. 20, 1938, twin (MC);
   m. Aug. 26, 1956 Marion Brown (MC), b.Feb.19,1939(MC).
   Children:
      MARVIN ANDREW-12 WEES,Jr., b.Feb.4,1958 (MC).
      HERBERT MATTHEW-12 WEES, b.March 23, 1964 (MC).
      MARION SUZANNE-12 WEES, b. Feb. 12, 1968 (MC).
MARTHA ANN-11 WEES, b. Jan. 20, 1938 (MC); twin (MC);
   m. Dec. 29, 1962 C. Robert Melberg, b. Oct.18,1927(MC).
   Children:
      CARL ROSS-12 MELBERG, b. Nov. 27, 1964 (MC).
      MARTHA ELIZABETH ANN-12 MELBERG, b. Oct. 23,1967(MC).

****

FRANK ROOSEVELT-10 SHAFFER (Ethel-9,Elizabeth-8, Asa-7, Asa-6,
                    James-5, Joseph-4, Joseph-3,
                    Robert-2, John-1)
b. Jan. 13, 1902 (MC);
d.
m(1)Oct. 15, 1924 Myrtle Vivienne Gabrielson, she was born
     on June 17, 1905 and died Aug. 5, 1956 (MC);
m(2)Aug. 23, 1958 Verna Krantz, she was born on April
     6, 1907 (MC).

     CHILDREN} (all by first marriage)

INFANT-11 SHAFFER, b.   ; d. "died" (MC).

BARBARA LOUISE-11 SHAFFER, b. Sept. 28, 1927 (MC);
   m. Feb.7,1948 Roy E. Pilcher, b.Nov.4,1926 (MC).
   Children:
      GARY LYNN-12 PILCHER, b. Nov. 29, 1948 (MC);
      MELANIE MARIE-12 PILCHER, b. April 24, 1960 (MC).
      AMY LUCINDA-12 PILCHER, b. April 26, 1961 (MC).
      IAN JAMES-12 PILCHER, b. May 19, 1963 (MC).

CAROL JOAN-11 SHAFFER, b. Jan. 7, 1933 (MC);
   m. Jan.22,1950 John Mills (MC).
   Children:
      DEBORAH CAROL-12 MILLS, b. Dec.25,1950 (MC).
      KIM JONATHAN-12 MILLS, b. April 24, 1954 (MC).
      DANIEL FRANK-12 MILLS, b. Aug. 9, 1957 (MC).
      LAURA BETH-12 MILLS, b. Nov. 21, 1958 (MC).

THOMAS GARY-11 SHAFFER, b. Aug. 8, 1941 (MC);
   m. June 27, 1964 Marilyn Apsege, b.Jan.10,1940 (MC).

****

Genealogy of the Crossman Family, Supplement #3 • ©1990 by Robert Owen Crossman • 908 Front • Conway, AR 72032

ELIZABETH JANE-10 SHAFFER,(Ethel-9, Elizabeth-8, Asa-7, Asa-6,
                    James-5, Joseph-4, Joseph-3,
                    Robert-2, John-1)
b. Aug. 5, 1914 (MC);
d.
m. June 26, 1937 Frederick Lott Oliver Griffith, he was
   born Feb. 24, 1908 and died July 2, 1967 (MC).

   CHILDREN:

ETHEL LEE-11 GRIFFITH, b. Aug. 18, 1942 (MC);
   m. June 24, 1961 Robert L. Rowe, b.April 30,1939 (MC).
   Children:
      YVONNE ELIZABETH-12 ROWE, b. Jan. 21, 1962 (MC).

ELLEN ANN-11 GRIFFITH, b. Oct. 6, 1945 (MC);
   m. May 22, 1965 James Pence, b.July 29,1945 (MC).
   Children:
      JAMES ALBERT FREDERICK-12 PENCE, b.Dec.24,1965(MC).

SARAH JANE-11 GRIFFITH, b. Nov. 13, 1949 (MC);
   m. Aug. 19, 1967 Lee Calvin Leonard, b.March 15,1946(MC).
   Children:
      LORI ANN-12 LEONARD, b. March 30, 1968 (MC).

****

Genealogy of the Crossman Family, Supplement #3 • ©1990 by Robert Owen Crossman • 908 Front • Conway, AR 72032

Our
Eleventh
Generation

see page
512

LAWRENCE-11 HICKS,   (Margaret-10, Mary-9, Mary-8, Asa-7,
            Asa-6, James-5, Joseph-4, Joseph-3,
            Robert-2, John-1)

b.
d.
m. Vesta Craig (MC).
   They lived in Indiana Co., PA (MC).

   CHILDREN:

MELVIN L.-12 HICKS, b.
    d.
    m. Dora Couveiso (MC).

WILLIAM BAIN-12 HICKS, b.
    d.
    m. Alice Ray (MC).

IONA-12 HICKS, b.
    d.
    m. George Norton (MC).

VELMA-12 HICKS, b.
    d.
    m. Phillip A. Saba (MC).

ERMA-12 HICKS, b.
    d.
    m. Francis R. Romasco (MC).

LAIRD W.-12 HICKS, b.
    d.
    m.

****

Genealogy of the Crossman Family, Supplement #3 • ©1990 by Robert Owen Crossman • 908 Front • Conway, AR 72032

see page
512

LEONARD GUY-11 HICKS   (Margaret-10, Mary-9, Mary-8, Asa-7,
                    Asa-6, James-5, Joseph-4, Joseph-3,
                    Robert-2, John-1)

b.
d.
m. Ida Summers (MC). They had two children.

    CHILDREN:

BLAINE G.-12 HICKS, b.
    d.
    m. Faye? _____?_____ (MC).

        CHILDREN:

            GERALD KEITH-13 HICKS, b. (MC)
                d.
                m.

DALE K.-12 HICKS, b.
    d.
    m. Hope? _____?_____(MC).

        CHILDREN:

            DALE ROBERT-13 HICKS, b.   (MC)
                d.
                m.

            RICHARD DeWAYNE-13 HICKS, b.   (MC)
                d.
                m.

****

LILLIAN-11 HICKS   (Margaret-10, Mary-9, Mary-8, Asa-7, Asa-6,
                     James-5, Joseph-4, Joseph-3,
                     Robert-2, John-1)

    b.
    d.
    m. Emaus Gould (MC).
        Lived in Redwood City, California (MC).

        CHILDREN:

    DOROTHY LOUISE-12 GOULD, b.   (MC)
        d.
        m.________Anderson (MC).

    JACQUELIN JOYCE-12 GOULD, b.   (MC)
        d.
        m. _________Karpeck (MC).

    KAREN ANN-12 GOULD, b.
        d.
        m._________Karpeck (MC).

****

see page
512

BESSIE V.-11 HICKS   (Margaret-10, Mary-9, Mary-8, Asa-7,
                Asa-6, James-5, Joseph-4, Joseph-3,
                Robert-2, John-1)

    b. April 12, 1888 (MC);
    d. June 10, 1970 (MC);
    m. William J. Kerr (MC).

    CHILDREN:

KENNETH MILLER-12 KERR, b. July 9, 1907 (MC);
    d. July 7, 1970 (MC);
    m. Gladys Judon (MC).
        Lived in Curvensville, PA (MC).

M. WILFRED-12 KERR, b.
    d.
    m.

H. VOGNE-12 KERR, b.
    d.
    m.

A MILES-12 KERR, b.
    d. Lived in Buffalo, N.Y. (MC).
    m.

VIOLES M.-12 KERR, b.
    d.
    m. Clyde Neal (MC); Lived in Pittsburg, PA (MC).

M. JEAN-12 KERR, b.
    d.
    m.Keith (MC); Lived in Buffalo, N.Y. (MC).

MILLICENT I.-12 KERR, b.
    d.
    m. Harold Wilson (MC); lived in New Bloomfield, PA(MC).

DOROTHY R.-12 KERR, b.
    d.
    m. Hauck (MC); lived in Niagra Falls, N.Y. (MC).

****

585

ALMA-11 HICKS   (Margaret-10, Mary-9, Mary-8, Asa-7, Asa-6,
                 James-5, Joseph-4, Joseph-3,
                 Robert-2, John-1)

      b.
      d.
      m. Raymond Martin (MC). They had three children.

         CHILDREN:

ANNA MARIE-12 MARTIN, b.
      d.
      m. Russell Smith (MC). They had two children.

         CHILDREN:

            MARYLYNN-13 SMITH, b. (MC)
               d.
               m.

            DAVID-13 SMITH, b.   (MC)
               d.
               m.

ETHEL ISABEL-12 MARTIN, b.   (MC)
      d.
      m.

VIRGINIA L.-12 MARTIN, b.   (MC)
      d.
      m.

                  ****

Genealogy of the Crossman Family, Supplement #3 • ©1990 by Robert Owen Crossman • 908 Front • Conway, AR 72032

VADA-11 HICKS   (Margaret-10, Mary-9, Mary-8, Asa-7, Asa-6,
                  James-5, Joseph-4, Joseph-3,
                  Robert-2, John-1)

b.
d.
m. Joseph Fetterhoff (MC).
   They lived in Plumville, Pennsylvania (MC).

   CHILDREN:

WILLIAM MONROE-12 FETTERHOFF, b.
   d.
   m. Jean Weaver (MC)
      They had two children: Garry and Jean Louise.(MC)

MILO WASHINGTON-12 FETTERHOFF, b.
   d.
   m. Grace Allison (MC).
      They had six children: James, Evelyn, Mildred,
      Barbara, Nancy Lee, and Otto Joe. (MC)

OTTO JOSEPH-12 FETTERHOFF, b.
   d.
   m. Ruth Stear (MC).
      They had three children: Laura Lee, George,
      Elizabeth.(MC).

JOSEPHINE-12 FETTERHOFF, b.
   d.
   m. Pavlck (MC).
      They had three children: Bonnie, James, and
      Donald (MC).

MAX-12 FETTERHOFF, b.
   d.
   m. Viola Lydic (MC).
      They had three children: Joseph, Kenneth, and Barry.

BETTY JANE-12 FETTERHOFF, b.
   d.
   m. William Loel (MC).
      They had one child: Darba Jo.

DONALD-12 FETTERHOFF, b.
   d.
   m.

****

ABRAM RALPH-11 HICKS   (Jessie-10, Elizabeth-9, Mary-8,
                        Asa-7, Asa-6, James-5, Joseph-4, Joseph-3,
                        Robert-2, John-1)

b. May 18, 1908 (MC);
d.
m. March 2, 1928 Mildred Emma Crawford (MC).

    CHILDREN:

SHIRLEY JEAN-12 HICKS, b.Sept. 11, 1928 (MC);
    d. March 8, 1946 (MC);
    m. Ervin (MC).

MARION LANG-12 HICKS, b. May 30, 1933 (MC);
    d. June 13, 1934 died in childhood (MC).

EDNA JOAN-12 HICKS, b. March 23, 1935 (MC);
    d.
    m.

CAROL LEE-12 HICKS, b. Oct. 28, 1938 (MC);
    d.
    m.

ALLEN RALPH-12 HICKS, b. May 7, 1940 (MC);
    d.
    m.

PAUL CRAWFORD-12 HICKS, b.Sept. 13, 1943 (MC);
    d.
    m.

OWEN BLAIR-12 HICKS, b. July 4, 1947 (MC);
    d.
    m.

****

Genealogy of the Crossman Family, Supplement #3 · ©1990 by Robert Owen Crossman · 908 Front · Conway, AR 72032

see page
541

WILLIAM RAY-11 HICKS   (Jessie-10, Elizabeth-9, Mary-8, Asa-7,
                  Asa-6, James-5, Joseph-4, Joseph-3,
                  Robert-2, John-1)

   b. March 27, 1907 (MC);
   d.
   m. June 16, 1935 Marjorie Emma Andrews (MC).

      CHILDREN:

WILLIAM ALLEN-12 HICKS, b. July 5, 1935 (MC);
     d. July 8, 1936 died in infancy (MC).

HAROLD ROGER-12 HICKS, b. Jan. 31, 1936 (MC).
     d.
     m.

LOIS ELAINE-12 HICKS, b. May 13, 1940 (MC).
     d.
     m.

EVA JOYCE-12 HICKS, b. July 11, 1942 (MC);
     d.
     m.

WILLIAM RAY-12 HICKS, b. Aug. 8, 1943 (MC).
     d.
     m.

****

Genealogy of the Crossman Family, Supplement #3 • ©1990 by Robert Owen Crossman • 908 Front • Conway, AR 72032

RUTH MAE-11 HICKS   (Jessie-10, Elizabeth-9, Mary-8, Asa-7,
                      Asa-6, James-5, Joseph-4, Joseph-3,
                      Robert-2, John-1)

b. April 25, 1909 (MC);
d.
m. Aug. 28, 1930 William Floyd Hoover (MC).

CHILDREN:

ALICE AILEEN-12 HOOVER, b. April 13, 1931 (MC);
    d.
    m. May 2, 1952 Richard B. Knox, he was born April
        9, 1931 (MC).
        CHILDREN:

            GRACE LEONA-13 KNOX, b.Feb.25,1953 (MC).
            ALICE MARIE-13 KNOX b. Feb. 24, 1954 (MC).
            WILLIAM STANLEY-13 KNOX, b.April 1, 1957 (MC).
            KEITH RICHARD-13 KNOX, b. Dec. 20, 1960 (MC).
            KEVIN LYNN-13 KNOX, b. Oct. 31, 1962 (MC).

RONALD EARL-12 HOOVER, b.Sept. 17, 1932 (MC);
    d.
    m. March 31, 1956 Martha Jean Sellers, she was born
        Sept. 16, 1934 (MC).

        CHILDREN:

            TIMOTHY EARL-13 HOOVER, b.June 19, 1958 (MC).
            TAMMY JEAN-13 HOOVER, b. July 7, 1960 (MC).
            THOMAS WILLIAM-13 HOOVER, b. Jan. 30, 1962 (MC).
            TABATHA LYNN-13 HOOVER, b. Oct. 2, 1968 (MC).

WILLIAM DALE-12 HOOVER, b. June 4, 1936 (MC);
    d.
    m. Sept.26, 1958 Wilma Ruth Lowry, she was born Sept.
        28, 1934 (MC).
        CHILDREN:
            SHERRY LYNN-13 HOOVER, b.Oct. 7, 1959 (MC).
            DONNA RUTH-13 HOOVER, b. Dec.20,1960 (MC).
            DALE WILLIAM-13 HOOVER, Jr., b.March 5, 1963 (MC).
            DENNIS WAYNE-13 HOOVER, b. June 19, 1964 (MC).

RUTH ANN-12 HOOVER, b. June 26, 1937 (MC);
    m.(1)Sept.10,1955 John Custer,Jr. he was b.Sept.10,1932;div.;
    m.(2)   Dale Worteringer (MC).
        CHILDREN:
            WESLEY FLOYD-13 CUSTER,b.May 30,1956; m.Sherrill (MC).
            WINONA ANN-13 CUSTER, b.June 10, 1957 (MC).
            VONDA LEA-13 CUSTER, b.Jan.29,1960 (MC).
            KIMBERLY KAY-13 CUSTER, b.Aug.21,1961 (MC).
            JAMES ALLEN-13 WORTERINTER, b.July 29, 1977 (MC).

SARAH JANE-12 HOOVER, b.Dec.4, 1940 (MC);
    m.Feb.11,1967 John W.Dinger, he was b.July 14,1935 (MC).
        CHILDREN:
            DONALD JAMES-13 DINGER, b.Feb.19,1973 (MC).
            JASON WILLIAM-13 DINGER, b.July 21,1977 (MC).

RUTH MAE-11 HICKS continued.

CHILDREN continued:

DONALD CHARLES-12 HOOVER, b. Aug. 15, 1942 (MC);
    m. April 22, 1962 Ione Esther Dunmire, she was born
    Aug. 24, 1943 (MC). They had three children.

CHILDREN:

GARY FLOYD-13 HOOVER, b. Feb. 19, 1943 (MC).

DONNETTE CHERYL-13 HOOVER, b.June 30, 1964 (MC).

DIANE-13 HOOVER, b. Dec. 31, 1967 (MC).

****

CARMEN E.-11 DEPP   (Melissa-10, Matilda-9, Mary-8, Asa-7.
                     Asa-6, James-5, Joseph-4, Joseph-3,
                      Robert-2, John-1)

b. Nov. 20, 1899 (MC);
d.
m. Nov. 9, 1919 George Sprankle, he was born in 1898 and
   he died in 1960 (MC).

   CHILDREN:

RONALD IRWIN-12 SPRANKLE, b.June 4,1920 (MC);
   m. May 16, 1946 Catherine Mayer, she was born April 26,1919(MC);
      CHILDREN:
         DOROTHY-13 SPRANKLE, b.Sept. 28, 1946 (MC).
         JAMES-13 SPRANKLE, b.Feb.20,1947 (MC).

NORMA-12 SPRANKLE, b.Oct.3,1921 (MC);
   m.Feb.8,1941 Clarence Barnett, he was born Feb.23,1920(MC).
      CHILDREN:
         JERRY-13 BARNETT,b.Aug.10,1941 (MC);
            m.Dolores Bivens, she was born July 19,1943 (MC).
               CHILDREN:
                  RONALD-14 BARNETT, b.Nov.23,1960 (MC).
                  MONICA-14 BARNETT, b.Nov.8,1963 (MC).
         WESLEY-13 BARNETT, b.Jan.20,1946 (MC).
         CARMEN JOANE-13 BARNETT, b.April 16,1943 (MC).

JAMES-12 SPRANKLE, b.April 19, 1924 (MC); unmarried (MC).

MERLE-12 SPRANKLE, b.Feb.21,1926 (MC);
   m.Aug. 1,1953 Sally White, she was born June 24,1935 (MC).
      CHILDREN:
         DEBORAH-13 SPRANKLE, b.March 20, 1954 (MC);
         LINDA-13 SPRANKLE, b. June 17, 1956 (MC);
         DOUGLAS-13 SPRANKLE, b. May 13, 1955 ? (MC).

NETTIE-12 SPRANKLE, b. May 31, 1928 (MC);
   m. Feb.21,1947 Harold Domb Jr., he was born Aug.25,19__(MC).
      CHILDREN:
         JOHN-13 DOMB, b.April 2, 1948 (MC).
         JUDITH-13 DOMB, b.Oct.9,1950 (MC).
         RONALD-13 DOMB, b.April 17, 1954 (MC).
         SANDRA-13 DOMB, b.March 28,1961 (MC).
         DONALD-13 DOMB, b.Oct.25,1963 (MC).

RICHARD-12 SPRANKLE, b.Dec.25,1931 (MC);
   m. Feb.14,1959 Emmy Lou Felton, she was born July 12,19__(MC).
      CHILDREN:
         KEITH-13 SPRANKLE, b.June 13, 1955 (MC).
         DANNY-13 SPRANKLE, b.July 28,1960 (MC).
         JEFFREY-13 SPRANKLE, b.April 20,1962 (MC).
         MARK-13 SPRANKLE, b.April 30,1964 (MC).

LARRY-12 SPRANKLE, b.Feb.2,1934 (MC);
   m.Dec.28,1958 Judith Ann Neil, she was born Sept.12,19__(MC).
      CHILDREN:
         JOSEPH-13 SPRANKLE, b.July 24,1959 (MC).
         JAMES-13 SPRANKLE, b. March 30, 1961 (MC).
ROBERT-12 SPRANKLE, b. Oct.17,1937 (MC);
   m.Jan.9,1959 Harriet Shrack, born Aug. 18,19__ (MC).
      CHILDREN:
         PATTY-13 SPRANKLE, b.Aug.28,1959 (MC).   592
         DONNA-13 SPRAKKLE, b.July 2,1963 (MC).
         DAVID-13 SPRANKLE, b.Aug.10,1965 (MC).

MARIE-11 SMITH   (Nannie-10, Everett-9, Asa-8, Asa-7, Asa-6,
                   James-5, Joseph-4, Joseph-3,
                   Robert-2, John-1)

    b. Nov. 11, 1918 Puxsutanny, PA (MC);
    d.
    m. March 20, 1939 Leslie Murray, he was born June 30,
       1918 (MC).

       CHILDREN:

    LESLIE JOSEPH-12 MURRAY, b.Jan.1,1940 (MC);
       m. 1958 Jacquin McConnaughey (MC).
       Children:
          LESLIE JOSEPH-13 MURRAY, III, b.   (MC).
          LYNN JEAN-13 MURRAY, b.   (MC).
          TINA MARIE-13 MURRAY, b.   (MC).
    JAMES GEORGE-12 MURRAY, b.July 22,1941 (MC);
       m.July 27,1959 Julian Sweeney (MC).
       Children:
          ALICIA-13 MURRAY, b.   (MC).
          PATRICK JOSEPH-13 MURRAY, b. (MC).
          BETH-13 MURRAY, b.   (MC).
          SHANNON-13 MURRAY, b.   (MC).
    PAUL THOMAS-12 MURRAY, b.Dec.5,1943 (MC);
       d.April 26, 1965 died overseas in service (MC).
    VICKI LEE-12 MURRAY, b.Sept.13,1947 (MC);
       m.(1) James Thomas Payne (MC); m.(2)_____ (MC).
       Children:
          JAMES THOMAS-13 PAYNE, b.   (MC).
          MARSHA IRENE-13 PAYNE, b.   (MC).
    ROBERT DALE-12 MURRAY, b.July 29,1949 (MC);
       m.March 4,1967 Bernice Johnston (MC).
       Children:
          LEAH-13 MURRAY, b.   (MC).
          JENNIFER FARA-13 MURRAY, b.   (MC)
    CHARLES-12 MURRAY, b. Feb. 2, 1951 (MC).

****

Information on this page supplied by Marion Croasmun of
Valier, PA in 1978,

see page
564

DONNA BELLE-11 EMHOFF   (Naomi-10, Isaac-9, Asa-8, Asa-7, Asa-6,
                James-5, Joseph-4, Joseph-3,
                Robert-2, John-1)

b. June 10, 1916 (MC);
d.
m. July 4, 1942 Clarence Eugene Postwaite (MC).

    CHILDREN:

JEANNE-12 POSTWAITE, b. April 22, 1943 (MC);
    m. April 23, 1965 Dennis Hallarn (MC).
    Children:
        DENNIS-13 HALLARN, b. Dec. 12, 1965 (MC).
        TARAI-13 HALLARN, b. Nov. 23, 1966 (MC).
        THOMAS-13 HALLARN, b. April , 1969 (MC).

MICHAEL JOHN-12 POSTWAITE, b. Dec. 3, 1944 (MC).

****

Information on this page supplied by Marion Croasmun of
Valier, PA in 1978.

ELLA MAE-11 EMHOFF (Naomi-10, Isaac-9, Asa-8, Asa-7, Asa-6,
        James-5, Joseph-4, Joseph-3,
        Robert-2, John-1)

b. May 23, 1917 (MC);
d.
m(1) Ernie Helm (MC);
m(2) March 23, 1939 John Pemberthy, he was born on Sept.
    28, 1916 (MC).

    CHILDREN:

DONNA MAE-12 HELM, b. June 16, 1933 (MC);
    m. Aug. 2, 1951 Robert Clark, born June 30,1928(MC).
    Children:
        ROBERT CHARLES-13 CLARK, b. Feb.11,1952 (MC).
        KAY-13 CLARK, b. Jan. 20, 1955 (MC).
        LYNN-13 CLARK, b. June 14, 1960 (MC).

JAMES LEE-12 HELM, b. Dec. 5, 1934 (MC).
    m. Cathy Barringer (MC).
    Children:
        LORI-13 HELM, b.   (MC).
        RICKY-13 HELM, b.   (MC).

JOHN NEWTON-12 PEMBERTHY, b. Aug. 30, 1942 (MC).
    m. Nannette Brogdon (MC).
    Children:
        DEAN-13 PEMBERTHY, b.   (MC).
        YVONNE-13 PEMBERTHY, b.   (MC).
        CHRISTOPHER-13 PEMBERTHY, b. (MC).

GENE ARTHUR-12 PEMBERTHY, b. Jan. 6, 1946 (MC);
    m. Marilyn Royer (MC).
    Children:
        SHAWN-13 PEMBERTHY, b.   (MC).
        KEITH-13 PEMBERTHY, b.   (MC).

****

Information on this page was supplied by Marion Croasmun of
Valier, PA in 1978.

Genealogy of the Crossman Family, Supplement #3 · ©1990 by Robert Owen Crossman · 908 Front · Conway, AR 72032

EILEEN-11 EMHOFF (Naomi-10, Isaac-9, Asa-8, Asa-7, Asa-6,
          James-5, Joseph-4, Joseph-3,
                    Robert-2, John-1)
  b. Sept. 14, 1918 (MC);
  d.
  m.   George Whitfield (MC).

     CHILDREN:

GEORGE-12 WHITFIELD, b.
     m. Rose________(MC).
     Children:
          KAREN-13 WHITFIELD, b.   (MC).

          DAVID-13 WHITFIELD, b.   (MC).

          PAUL-13 WHITFIELD, b.   (MC).

          RONALD-13 WHITFIELD, b.   (MC).

BRENDA-12 WHITFIELD, b.
     m. Charles Taylor (MC).
     Children:
          TRACY-13 TAYLOR, b.   (MC).

          CHARLES-13 TAYLOR, b.   (MC).

LARRY-12 WHITFIELD, b.
     m. Judy________(MC).
     Children:
          KENNETH ALLEN-13 WHITFIELD, b. (MC).

          BRIAN-13 WHITFIELD, b.   (MC).

                    ****

Information on this page supplied by Marion Croasmun of
Valier, PA in 1978.

see page
564

WANDA-11 EMHOFF (Naomi-10, Isaac-9, Asa-8, Asa-7, Asa-6,
                  James-5, Joseph-4, Joseph-3,
                  Robert-2, John-1)
b. April 24, 1921 (MC);
d.
m(1)   Milford Evans, they divorced (MC);
m(2) Aug. 15, 1972 Paul Jordon (MC).

        CHILDREN:

MILFORD JOSEPH-12 EVANS, b. July 7, 1937 (MC);
    m. Rose Mary______(MC).
    Children:
      ANTHONY-13 EVANS, b.   (MC).
      PATRICIA-13 EVANS, b.   (MC).
      JOE-13 EVANS, b.   (MC).
      ROSE MARIE-13 EVANS, b.   (MC).
PATRICIA LOU-12 EVANS, b. June 7, 1940 (MC);
    m. Gus Hutmire
    Children:
      TIMOTHY-13 HUTMIRE, b.   (MC).
      TERRI-13 HUTMIRE, b. Aug. 22, 1960, twin (MC).
      SHERRI-13 HUTMIRE, b. Aug. 22, 1960, twin (MC).
      WENDY-13 HUTMIRE, b.   (MC).
      TRACIE-13 HUTMIRE, b.   (MC).
BARBARA KAY-12 EVANS, b. Oct. 4, 1943 (MC);
    m. Henry Walker (MC).
    Children:
      LISA-13 WALKER, b.   (MC).
      KIM-13 WALKER, b.   (MC).
      BRUCE-13 WALKER, b.   (MC).
DONALD JOHN-12 EVANS, b. Feb. 25, 1947 (MC);
    m. Joyce Bhe (MC).
    Children:
      DONALD-13 EVANS, b.   (MC).
ROBERT LEROY-12 EVANS, b. Feb. 29, 1948 (MC);
    m. Paula Hinkle (MC).
    Children:
      ROBERT-13 EVANS, b.   (MC).
      KIM-13 EVANS, b.   (MC).
      BRIAN-13 EVANS, b.   (MC).

                ****

Information on this page supplied by Marion Croasmun of
Valier, PA in 1978.

see page
564

JOHN "Jack"-11 EMHOFF (Naomi-10, Isaac-9, Asa-8, Asa-7,
                Asa-6, James-5, Joseph-4, Joseph-3,
                Robert-2. John-1)
    b. Nov. 2, 1922 (MC);
    d.
    m. Nov. 28, 1942 Martha Benson, born July 24, 1919 (MC).

    CHILDREN:

JOHN DENNIS 'Jack'-12 EMHOFF, b. March 22, 1944 (MC);
    m. June 6, 1964 Sally Hanneman, born July 18,1941(MC).
    Children:
        TRACIE-13 EMHOFF, b. Dec. 30, 1965 (MC).
        DENNIS-13 EMHOFF, b. Dec. 8, 1967 (MC).
        MICHELLE-13 EMHOFF, b. March 8, 1970 (MC).

BRUCE ALLEN-12 EMHOFF, b. Aug. 22, 1946 (MC);
    m. Sept. 23, 1967 Cynthia Corbin, born Jan.9,1950(MC).
    Children:
        MICHAEL-13 EMHOFF, b. May 5, 1970 (MC).

KAREN ANN-12 EMHOFF, b. April 15, 1951 (MC);
    m. Sept. 19, 1970 Edward D. Hollis (MC).
    Children:
        MATTHEW ERIN-13 HOLLIS, b. May   , 1975 (MC).

MARSHA LEE-12 EMHOFF, b. Dec. 17, 1957 (MC).

                ****

Information on this page supplied by Marion Croasmun of
Valier, PA in 1978.

"...the farm of Asa and Patience and their grave..."
From tombstones:

Asa Croasmun
Died May 29, 1828
aged 63 years

Patience Croasmun
Died June 27, 1828
aged 63 years

Children born unto Asa Crosman and wife
Cloe Crosman   born Sept. 12   1792.
[...]a Crosman   born Oct. 15   1794
Rebekah Crosman   born Sept. 5   1796
Joseph Crosman   born Sept 12   1798

"A copy of what serves as a birth certificate for
Asa & Patience children from the archives of New Hampshire."

Front row (left to right)
Jim Chambers; James Croasmun; Miles Croasmun; Asa Croasmun; Nathan Croasmun; Isaac Croasmun   SEE PAGE 491
Back row (left to right)
Lizzie C. Chambers; Mary Croasmun; Margaret Beck Croasmun; Mary Robinson Croasmun; Rachel Mary Dennison Blose Croasmun

50th Reunion Croasmun Picture

INDEX OF NAMES

Prepared by
Dale F. Croasmun

202 Sunset Drive • Cumberland, MD 21502
[See also Croasman, Croasmun and Crossman]

**I must express my deep appreciation
to
Dale F. Croasmun**

[202 Sunset Drive • Cumberland, MD 21502]

for this index of names.

**Additional copies of this genealogy
may be purchased from
Bob Crossman
bcrossman@arumc.org
8 Sternwheel Drive
Conway, AR 72034-9391**

Genealogy of the Croasmun Family, Supplement #3 • ©1998 by Robert Owen Croasmun • 908 Front Street • Conway, Arkansas 72032

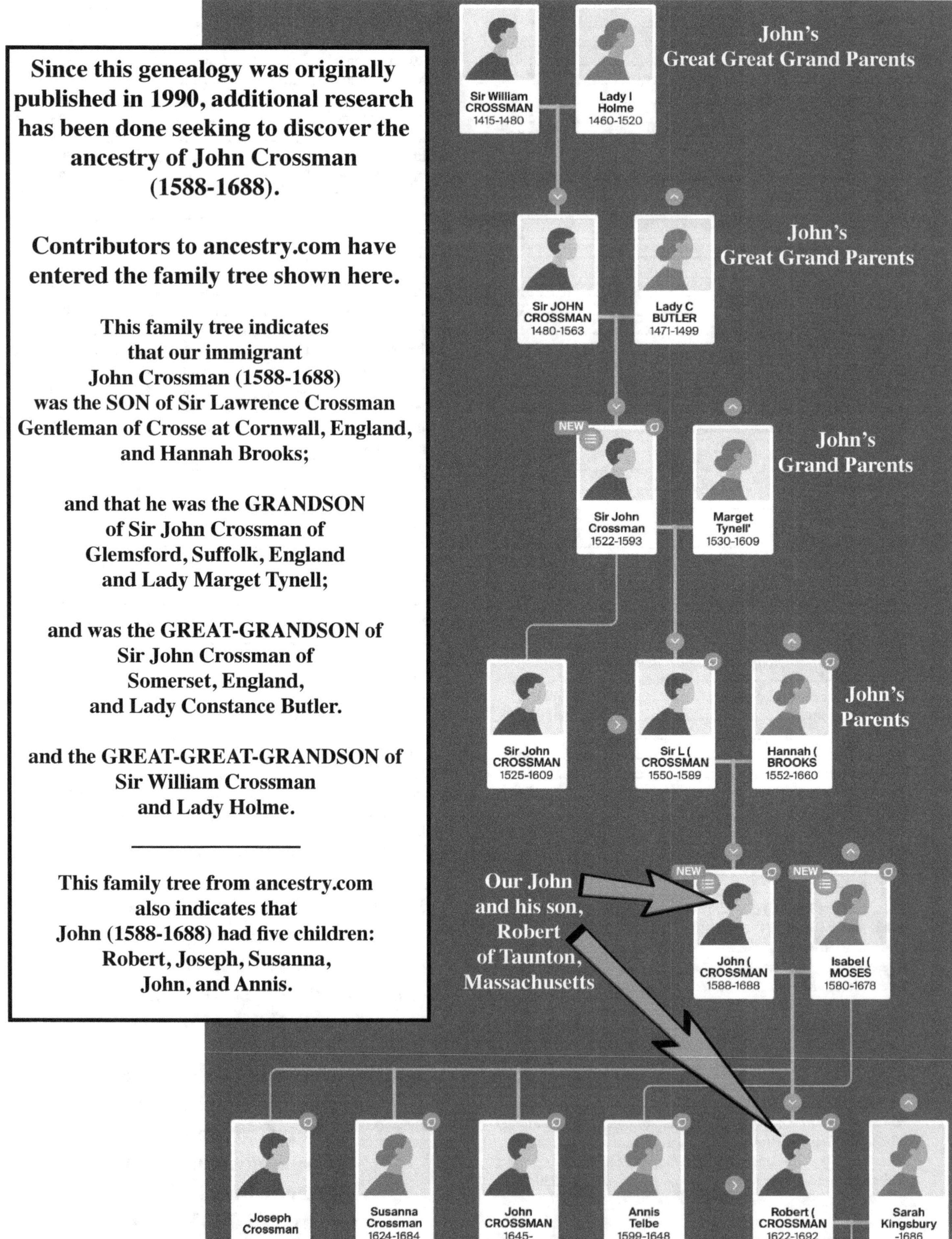

Since this genealogy was originally published in 1990, additional research has been done seeking to discover the ancestry of John Crossman (1588-1688).

Contributors to ancestry.com have entered the family tree shown here.

This family tree indicates that our immigrant John Crossman (1588-1688) was the SON of Sir Lawrence Crossman Gentleman of Crosse at Cornwall, England, and Hannah Brooks;

and that he was the GRANDSON of Sir John Crossman of Glemsford, Suffolk, England and Lady Marget Tynell;

and was the GREAT-GRANDSON of Sir John Crossman of Somerset, England, and Lady Constance Butler.

and the GREAT-GREAT-GRANDSON of Sir William Crossman and Lady Holme.

This family tree from ancestry.com also indicates that John (1588-1688) had five children: Robert, Joseph, Susanna, John, and Annis.

John's Great Great Grand Parents
Sir William CROSSMAN 1415-1480
Lady I Holme 1460-1520

John's Great Grand Parents
Sir JOHN CROSSMAN 1480-1563
Lady C BUTLER 1471-1499

John's Grand Parents
NEW
Sir John Crossman 1522-1593
Marget Tynell' 1530-1609

John's Parents
Sir John CROSSMAN 1525-1609
Sir L (CROSSMAN 1550-1589
Hannah (BROOKS 1552-1660

Our John and his son, Robert of Taunton, Massachusetts
NEW
John (CROSSMAN 1588-1688
NEW
Isabel (MOSES 1580-1678

Joseph Crossman
Susanna Crossman 1624-1684
John CROSSMAN 1645-
Annis Telbe 1599-1648
Robert (CROSSMAN 1622-1692
Sarah Kingsbury -1686